Marcela Depiante

Indefinites

Marcela Depiante
445 Whitney Rd. Ext. H-209
Storrs, CT 06269
U.S.A

Linguistic Inquiry Monographs
Samuel Jay Keyser, general editor

Indefinites   Molly Diesing

The MIT Press
Cambridge, Massachusetts
London, England

This book was set in Times Roman by Asco Trade Typesetting Ltd., Hong Kong, and was printed and bound in the United States of America.

Library of Congress Cataloging-in-Publication Data
Diesing, Molly.
    Indefinites / Molly Diesing.
        p.   cm.—(Linguistic inquiry monographs; 20)
    Includes bibliographical references and index.
    ISBN 0-262-04131-6 (hc).—ISBN 0-262-54066-5 (pbk.)
    1. Grammar, Comparative and general—Syntax. 2. Definiteness
    (Linguistics) 3. Semantics. 4. Grammar, Comparative and
    general—Quantifiers. 5. Government-binding theory (Linguistics)
    6. Grammar, Comparative and general—Noun phrase. I. Title.
    II. Series. P291.D54   1992
    415—dc20   91-45987
                                                                          CIP

To my parents

Contents

Contents

Series Foreword

We are pleased to present this monograph as the twentieth in the series *Linguistic Inquiry Monographs*. These monographs will present new and original research beyond the scope of the article, and we hope they will benefit our field by bringing to it perspectives that will stimulate further research and insight.

Originally published in limited edition, the *Linguistic Inquiry Monograph* series is now available on a much wider scale. This change is due to the great interest engendered by the series and the needs of a growing readership. The editors wish to thank the readers for their support and welcome suggestions about future directions the series might take.

Samuel Jay Keyser
for the Editorial Board

Preface

This book is a revision of my doctoral dissertation, completed at the University of Massachusetts at Amherst in September, 1990. Although I have retained the overall structure and organization of the original, within each chapter I have made numerous substantive revisions and additions. In chapter 2 I have added some discussion of the relationship between focus and NP interpretation. I have expanded the discussions of both presupposition accommodation and specificity in chapter 3 and have re-worked much of the analysis in chapter 4. Finally, I have expanded the introductory chapter in the hopes of providing a theoretical introduction to the syntactic and semantic frameworks assumed here that will be useful to a wide range of readers.

The list of people who have offered me comments and criticisms during the various stages of completing this work is rather long, but I'd like to single out a few of them for special thanks. Angelika Kratzer and David Pesetsky have been of central influence from beginning to end, both through their comments and suggestions, and through the example set by their own scholarship and high standards. Among those who have read and extensively commented on earlier versions are F. Roger Higgins, Manfred Krifka, Robert May, Arnim von Stechow, and Koichi Tateishi. I would also like to thank Andy Barss, Maria Bittner, Mürvet Enç, Irene Heim, Eloise Jelinek, Kyle Johnson, Dick Oehrle, Barbara Partee, and Wolfgang Sternefeld. The students in my Spring 1991 colloquium seminar at the University of Arizona provided much lively discussion and also helped me remedy at least some of the expressive defects. I have also benefited from the comments and questions of audiences at Swarthmore College, The University of Arizona, the University of California at Irvine, the University of Wisconsin-Madison, the University of Toronto, the 1989 LSA Meeting in Washington, D.C., and the 1990–1991 LSA Meeting in Chicago. An earlier version of part of chapter 2 appears in *Linguistic Inquiry* 23.3.

I would also like to express my gratitude for the financial assistance I have received from various sources, including a "Javits grant" (D/ED G008641012) from the U.S. Department of Education, research support from an NSF grant (BNS 87-19999) awarded to Emmon Bach, Angelika Kratzer, and Barbara Partee, and a fellowship from the University of Massachusetts. Finally, I would like to thank Anne Mark for her expert editorial work in the final preparation of the manuscript.

Indefinites

Chapter 1
Deriving Logical
Representations: A Proposal

1.1 Introduction

The main concern of this monograph is an interdisciplinary one: I investigate the relationship between the syntactic and semantic representations of sentences within the framework of generative grammar. In particular, I address the problem of deriving logical representations from the syntactic representations of sentences, focusing primarily on the issues of quantification (that is, the representation of the relative scope of operators and the determination of quantificational force) and the interpretation of indefinites. In doing this, I concentrate on two central questions, drawing primarily on data from English and German:

(1) What are the possible semantic interpretations of indefinite and quantificational NPs?

(2) What role does the syntactic representation play in the derivation of the semantic representation of NPs?

Although the syntactic representation of scope relations is a familiar concept (see May 1977), determining the quantificational force of an NP may at first blush appear to be purely an interpretive question concerning the semantics of determiners and the like, with the syntactic structure of the sentence playing no role. My aim here is to show that purely syntactic concerns such as word order and hierarchical structure do in fact play an important role in the process of "reading off" semantic representations of NPs from the syntactic forms of sentences. In other words, I am concerned primarily with developing an account of the interface between syntactic theory and semantic theory.

Specifically, I propose a means of relating a primarily syntactic theory, the Government-Binding Theory of Chomsky (1981) and others, with the

semantic theory of NP interpretation developed by Kamp (1981) and
Heim (1982). In the analysis I propose, one of the contributions of purely
syntactic configurations to the derivation of Kamp-Heim logical representations is stated in terms of a simple mapping algorithm that divides the
syntactic tree into two parts, which have correlates in their associated
"semantic partition"—the logical representation in which the scope and
quantificational force of NPs is represented.

Before I proceed, some introductory background is necessary. In the
next two sections I present the basics of the syntactic and semantic frameworks that I take as my starting point in this work.

1.2   The Syntactic Roots of Indefinite Interpretations

The basic syntactic framework I will be assuming is that of Government-
Binding Theory, as developed by Chomsky (1981, 1986a, 1986b) and
others. I will not undertake to present a comprehensive overview of the
theory here (a more thorough introduction can be found in Haegeman
1991), but will instead focus on two major components that are central to
the main thesis of this monograph. The first concerns a recent develop-
ment in the theory of phrase structure. A number of works on phrase
structure have converged on the hypothesis that the subject of a sentence
can be base-generated within the verb projection (the VP). This yields a
system of X-bar-theoretic phrase structure rules that differs somewhat
from the original phrase structure rules as stated in Chomsky 1986a. The
revised clause structure posits two possible positions for the subject within
the X-bar phrase structure. I will refer to this proposal as the *VP-Internal
Subject Hypothesis*.

As illustrated by the tree in (3), one subject position is situated as in the
original *Barriers* framework (Chomsky 1986a), dominated immediately by
IP (the [Spec, IP], or *IP subject*). The other subject position is located
within the VP. I assume that this VP-internal subject position is the
[Spec, VP] (referred to alternatively as the *VP subject*).

(3) *The VP-Internal Subject Hypothesis*

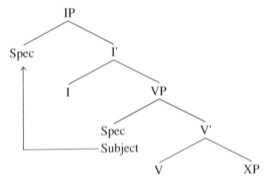

As indicated by the arrow in (3), the subject in a sentence such as (4) is base-generated within the VP in the [Spec, VP] position and subsequently raises at S-structure to the [Spec, IP] position.

(4) Walter plays the contrabassoon.

An essential consequence of the VP-Internal Subject Hypothesis (and one of the theoretical arguments in its favor) is that subjects are θ-marked within the VP, allowing an attractive simplification of θ-theory.

This structure has been proposed in a large number of different analyses to account for a correspondingly diverse range of phenomena (see Koopman and Sportiche 1985, Fukui and Speas 1986, Kuroda 1988, Pollock 1989, Diesing 1990a, Chomsky 1991, among many others). Since detailed arguments for the structure in (3) are given in these works and elsewhere, I will simply take the VP-Internal Subject Hypothesis as given.

One of the questions I wish to address in this monograph concerns the properties of the two subject positions. Namely, is there any difference (other than relative position) between a VP-internal subject and a VP-external subject? Does the VP have any properties that distinguish it from IP, and vice versa?[1] In this work I approach these questions by investigating the hypothesis that the VP and the area "outside" of VP (at the IP level) are distinct domains for different kinds of quantification, and that therefore IP subjects and VP subjects are distinguished in the derivations of the logical representations of sentences. Put in another way, the two subject positions are distinguished in the mapping from S-structure to logical representations.

It may not be immediately obvious what role the syntactic structures of IP and VP can play in the semantics of quantified structures. Therefore, at this point it is necessary to introduce another component of the Government-

Binding Theory: the level of logical form. The idea that the syntactic structure of a sentence can play a role in determining logical representations (scope relations in particular) has led Government-Binding theorists to posit an abstract intermediate syntactic level of logical form (LF) that mediates in the mapping from syntax to logical representations (May 1985).[2] Just as S-structure is the level to which the phonological interpretations may be assigned, LF is the level from which the semantic interpretations are assigned. In parallel to the derivation of S-structure from D-structure, LF is a phrase structure representation that is derived from S-structure by the application of syntactic rules. Thus, the intermediate LF representations are modeled on their S-structure syntactic representations.

The LF movement rules fall under the general theory of transformational mappings as processes that can be subsumed under the form of the general Move α schema of Chomsky (1981). A central case of LF movement is the rule of *quantifier raising* (QR), which raises quantificational NPs to adjoin to IP, producing a structure in which an operator (that is, the quantificational NP) binds a variable (the trace left by the application of QR). The quantifier phrase in its adjoined position thus marks the scope of the quantifier in that its scope is the set of nodes c-commanded by the raised NP at LF. The result is of course not the final semantic representation. Within the Government-Binding framework, the LF level is regarded as intermediary between the syntax and the logical representations. It is from this abstract level of syntactic representation that the actual logical representations are derived. I make here the additional claim that it is at this level that the VP-internal and VP-external subject positions can be distinguished with respect to quantification.

There is a derivational "step" that still remains to be specified. A procedure is needed to indicate how the syntactic LF representation gets mapped into the logical representations (using here those of the type developed by Kamp and Heim). In explicating the derivation of the semantic representations of sentences from syntactic representations, I depend on the notion of a *semantic partition* of a sentence, in particular a type of partitioning developed in the theories of NP interpretation proposed by Kamp (1981) and Heim (1982). I initially propose to relate this semantic framework to syntactic structures such as that shown in (3) by an algorithm that splits the syntactic tree into two parts, corresponding to the major division (or partition) in the semantic representation.

1.3 Semantic Partition and the Interpretation of Indefinites

The idea of dividing a sentence into two parts on semantic and/or pragmatic grounds is by no means new. The notion of such partition has also taken a number of different forms throughout time, embodying intrasentential distinctions such as topic and comment, theme and rheme (e.g., Daneš 1964, Firbas 1970), and subject and predicate. The division I am concerned with arises in analyses of restrictive quantification (particularly the analyses of Lewis (1975) and those following him). Using the terminology of Heim (1982), I refer to this division as the *restrictive clause/nuclear scope partition*. I focus mainly on the derivation of this partition at the sentence level, and then go on to consider some of its applications in the syntax-semantics interface.

1.3.1 A Brief Introduction to the Kamp-Heim Theory

In order to explain what the nature of the restrictive clause/nuclear scope partition is, I give here a brief introduction to the Kamp-Heim approach to the semantics of NPs. (This introduction is by no means complete; see, for example, Heim 1982 for a detailed exposition of the theory and the motivations that lie behind it.) In this introduction I concentrate on a few simple sentences to show by example how the restrictive clause/nuclear scope division functions at the sentence level.

A primary motivation for the Kamp-Heim theory is based on observations concerning the quantificational variability of indefinites (originally made by Lewis (1975)) that preclude their being analyzed as existential quantifiers (as proposed by Russell (1919)). The following sentences, with their paraphrases (given in the (b) examples), illustrate how indefinites can vary in quantificational force depending on the context in which they appear:

(5) a. A contrabassoonist usually plays too loudly.
    b. Most contrabassoonists play too loudly.

(6) a. Cellists seldom play out of tune.
    b. Few cellists play out of tune.

(7) a. If a violist plays a solo, the audience often leaves the room.
    b. In many of the situations in which a violist plays a solo, the audience leaves the room.

The sentences in (5)–(7) show that rather than being simply existentially quantified, indefinites can take their quantificational force from other elements in the sentence (such as adverbs like *usually*, *seldom*, and *often*).

To account for these observations, Heim claims that indefinites are not inherently quantified, but merely introduce variables into the logical representation. (I will refer mainly to Heim's work in the examples that follow, but most, if not all, of what I say is applicable to Kamp's theory as well.) To illustrate how this works, I will begin with a simple case:

(8) a. A man owns a llama.

    b. $(\exists_{x,y})$ [x is a man $\land$ y is a llama $\land$ x owns y]

In (8a) the indefinite NPs *a man* and *a llama* are not represented as existential quantifiers; rather, they introduce variables. Another way of expressing this is to say that indefinites have no quantificational force of their own. They must receive quantificational force by being bound by some other operator. In this case there is no other quantificational element in the sentence that can function as the adverbs do in (5)–(7). Here the variable introduced by the indefinite is bound by an implicit existential quantifier that "existentially" closes off the nuclear scope, preventing the occurrence of unbound variables. In the case of the sentence in (8) the nuclear scope simply contains all instances of the variables introduced by the indefinites in a sentence. This can be seen in the logical representation given in (8b). The implicit existential quantifier is shown within parentheses, and it binds all the variables (in this case x and y) within the nuclear scope, which for purposes of illustration is enclosed within brackets. (I will dispense with unnecessary parentheses and brackets in the discussions that follow.)

The logical representation in (8b) can also be represented graphically in the "box notation" employed by Kamp (1981), which I present in (9).[3] The box represents the domain of existential closure, or the nuclear scope.

(9) *Nuclear scope*

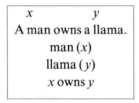

The example in (8) illustrates the simplest case involving the interpretation of NPs, which involves only simple indefinites. Only a nuclear scope is formed, and the only quantificational (in the sense of variable binding)

operation involved is existential closure. No restrictive clause is required in the logical representation shown in (8b). Thus, although every sentence undergoes the process of being mapped into logical representations, not every sentence ends up being divided into both a restrictive clause and a nuclear scope. In other words, the mapping to the semantic representation (however it is formulated) can in some cases yield a one-part representation. To see how restrictive clause formation works in Heim's framework, we need to consider a slightly more complicated case involving the interpretation of quantified NPs, such as the one shown in (10).

(10) a. Every llama ate a banana.
  b. Every$_x$ [x is a llama]   ($\exists_y$) y is a banana $\wedge$ x ate y
         ↑   ↑   ↑
     quantifier   restrictive clause   nuclear scope

An important property of quantifiers like *every* is that they quantify over a restricted set. The sentence in (10a) is true if and only if for all value assignments to the variable x that make the restrictive clause true, there is an assignment to the variable y that makes the nuclear scope true.[4] Thus, in (10a) the quantifier *every* quantifies not over every *thing*, but over every thing that is a llama. This restriction on the quantifier is given an explicit representation in the restrictive clause ([x is a llama]), as shown in (10b). The restrictive clause simply specifies the set that the quantifier quantifies over. The variables introduced by the NPs in (10a) are bound in the following way: the quantifier *every* binds all the variables that are established in the restrictive clause (the variable x in this case). Existential closure in turn binds all the remaining variables introduced in the nuclear scope (such as the variable y introduced by *a banana* in (10)).

In Kamp's box notation, restrictive clause formation can be represented as *box splitting*, as in (11).

(11) *Box splitting*

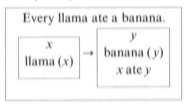

In this notation, the division of the sentence is represented by the embedded boxes. The left-hand, or antecedent, box corresponds to the restrictive clause, and the right-hand, or consequent, box corresponds to the nuclear scope.

The tripartite form exemplified in (10) also provides a means of representing the interpretations of the indefinites that are apparently bound by quantificational adverbs, such as the ones in (5)–(7). Here the variables introduced by the indefinites are introduced in a restrictive clause, and the quantificational adverb serves as the operator binding the variables, thereby giving them quantificational force:

(12) a. Usually$_x$ [x is a contrabassonist] x plays loudly
    b. Seldom$_x$ [x is a cellist] x plays out of tune

From the representations in (12) it is clear how the quantificational variability of indefinites can arise. The number of true variable assignments to the indefinite required to make the sentence true depends on the choice of adverb.

The Kamp-Heim theory of NP interpretation is thus formulated in terms of *restricted quantification*, in which the domain of the quantifier is established by the restrictive clause.[5] To summarize this approach, in the Kamp-Heim theory indefinites are represented as variables, which are unselectively bound by abstract operators like existential closure, or overt operators like the quantifier *every*. Quantifiers like *every* introduce a restriction (which is represented by restrictive clause formation or box splitting). The resulting logical representations take a tripartite form consisting of an operator, a restrictive clause, and the nuclear scope, as shown in (10b).

Even with only the most elementary introduction, it should be clear that one of the main questions that arise in applying restricted quantification to natural language is how to determine the restrictive clause. In other words, how is the sentence divided into the "semantic partition" consisting of the restrictive clause and the nuclear scope? In the next section I will sketch a proposal for answering this question, and the bulk of this work will be devoted to motivating and supporting this hypothesis.

1.3.2 The Next Step: Deriving the Logical Representations

In this section I begin to consider the question of how sentences are divided into the restrictive clause and the nuclear scope in the mapping from S-structure to the logical representations. This is basically the question of what role the syntactic structure of a sentence (as described by the X-bar phrase structures introduced in section 1.2) can play in determining the interpretation of the NPs contained within it. In other words, how are the variables introduced by NPs to be mapped from the syntactic positions of NPs into nuclear scopes and restrictive clauses? Or stated in terms of box notation, what is the "box-splitting" algorithm?

For the purposes of this introduction, I limit myself to the question of where *subjects* are mapped, ignoring for the moment the issues involved in the interpretation of objects and adjuncts and such. The interpretation of objects will be dealt with in chapters 3 and 4. I will also limit myself to considering only the syntactic determinants of the partition. Therefore, I will not consider at this point the possible contributions of apparently nonsyntactic factors such as focus and intonation. This is not to deny that these factors are relevant, as the purely syntactic structure of a sentence is not the *only* determinant of semantic partition. I will discuss the role of focus to some extent in later chapters, but at this point it is instructive to concentrate on one particular phenomenon in order to clearly present the basic outlines of my approach.

In the chapters that follow, I propose and explore a fairly close syntactic link between the two-subject clause structure (the VP-Internal Subject Hypothesis) presented in section 1.2 and the Kamp-Heim-style tripartite logical representations introduced in section 1.3.1. This link, or interface, between the syntactic representation and the semantic representation takes the form of a mapping procedure that splits the syntactic tree into two parts. The two parts of the sentence are then mapped into the two major parts of the logical representation, the restrictive clause and the nuclear scope, producing the desired semantic partition.

The procedure works as follows: Assuming a two-subject model of phrase structure, divide the sentence into a restrictive clause and a nuclear scope as shown in (13) (for the purposes of exposition, assume that this splitting takes place at the level of LF).

(13) *Mapping Hypothesis (tree splitting)*

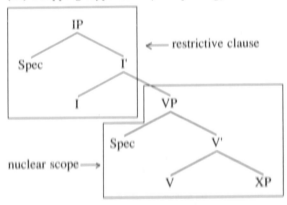

In (13) the two-subject tree is divided into two parts (outlined by boxes for purposes of illustration), one consisting of the VP, and the other consisting of the subtree dominating the VP (which I will refer to as the *IP-level structure*). My claim is that the *tree-splitting* process illustrated in (13) corresponds to box splitting in the Kamp-style box notation (see (11)). Expressed in words, the derivation of the representations shown in (13) is as follows:

(14) *Mapping Hypothesis*
    Material from VP is mapped into the nuclear scope.
    Material from IP is mapped into a restrictive clause.

The diagram in (13) can be intuitively thought of as the two-subject tree from (3) with the split boxes from the diagram in (11) superimposed upon it (where the boxes in (13) correspond to the embedded split boxes in (11)).

At this point some clarification concerning the representations in (8) and (10) is in order. I have claimed that the two parts of the split tree correspond to the two major parts of the logical representation, the restrictive clause and the nuclear scope. Of course, there is a third part in the logical representation, which is the quantifier itself. If the syntactic level of LF involves IP-adjoined quantifier phrases, there must still be a means of excluding the actual quantifier from both the restrictive clause and the nuclear scope. This issue is actually taken up by Heim. In deriving LF representations, Heim (1982, chap. 2) proposes a rule in addition to QR (which she calls "Quantifier Construal"), which adjoins every *quantifier* to S, or IP (following her QR-like rule of "NP-Prefixing"). This leads to a truly "tripartite tree," as shown in (15) for the sentence *Every llama arrived.*

(15) *Heim-style LF representation (updated)*

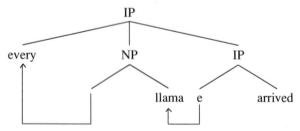

Thus, in Heim's derivation there are two adjunction operations. The NP-Prefixing rule raises the NP *every llama* out of IP, and then the Quantifier Construal rule moves *every* out of the NP to adjoin to IP itself. The Quantifier Construal rule is also used in deriving the logical representations of sentences with quantificational adverbs:

(16) a. Cellists seldom play out of tune.
     b. seldom$_x$ [x is a cellist] x plays out of tune

In sentences such as (16a) the quantificational adverb takes sentential scope. This interpretation can be derived by adjoining the adverb to IP through the rule of Quantifier Construal. In the remainder of this monograph I will not concern myself further with the more articulated LF representation shown in (15), but will continue to use the representations in (8) and (10) as a form of shorthand for the representation in (15), with the assumption that some Quantifier Construal rule operates to separate the quantifier from the other two parts of the logical representation.

The Mapping Hypothesis establishes a straightforward relationship between syntactic structure and the form of the logical representations. Thus, the semantic partition of a sentence into a restrictive clause part and a nuclear scope part has its "syntactic roots" in the two-subject structure in (3), through the process in (13).

1.4 Syntactic Factors in the Semantics of NPs: A Preview

The Mapping Hypothesis proposed in (13) has the virtues of being simple and intuitively straightforward. The next step is to show that it is empirically well motivated as well. If the relationship between the syntactic and semantic representations is as straightforward as suggested by (13), this should be reflected in interactions between syntactic phenomena and the semantic interpretation(s) of NPs. In the chapters that follow I examine a range of empirical phenomena in syntax and semantics that demonstrate that there is in fact a connection between the syntax of a sentence and its logical representation of the sort illustrated in (13).

Chapter 2 is devoted to motivating the basic workings of the Mapping Hypothesis. I examine data from English and German that provide empirical support for the tree-splitting procedure. The supporting argument consists of several parts. In the first part I show that the two possible positions for the subject in the semantic representation do in fact correspond to two possible interpretations of the subject. These two interpretations are highlighted by a contrast in interpretation of bare plural subjects (noted originally by Carlson (1977b)) between temporary-state predicates (Carlson's stage-level predicates) and permanent-state (individual-level) predicates. I show that this contrast between the two types of predicates is actually syntactic in nature, but because of the workings of the Mapping

Hypothesis, it is reflected also in the available semantic interpretations of a bare plural subject.

Next, I show that the two syntactic subject positions posited in the VP-Internal Subject Hypothesis can be distinguished at S-structure in German. The German data show that the two subject positions are differentiated syntactically with respect to extraction operations. Finally, I show that the two syntactic subject positions correspond to the two positions in the semantic representations, as predicted by the Mapping Hypothesis. One major consequence of this chapter is that it appears that German and English are rather different in that in German the tree-splitting algorithm seems to reflect the S-structure word order of the sentence, whereas in English abstract LF movement operations are clearly involved.

In chapter 3 I extend the idea of deriving the Heim-style representations by the Mapping Hypothesis to the interpretation of quantified NPs. The central question of this chapter is that stated in (2): What are the possible interpretations of indefinite and quantified NPs? One major consequence of the data and analysis I present is that indefinites are not all treated uniformly. Specifically, I differentiate two types of indefinites, those that induce box splitting and those that do not (see also Partee 1988 for a discussion of the ambiguity of indefinites with the determiners *few* and *many*). This is a shift from the Kamp-Heim position in which all indefinites are treated uniformly as variables. I show that this differential treatment of indefinites is based on the contrast between presuppositional and cardinal determiners noted by Milsark (1974).

I also extend this analysis to the problem of quantifier scope determination. By differentiating the two interpretations *syntactically* with respect to the Mapping Hypothesis, I show that scope order preferences of quantifiers can be represented straightforwardly within a syntactic theory of quantifier scope. In investigating the connection between the two types of interpretations for indefinites and the derivation of the level of LF via the rule of quantifier raising (QR) in the sense of May (1977, 1985), I show that there is a relationship between presuppositionality and the obligatoriness of QR. This association is supported by data from English concerning a special case of VP-deletion, antecedent-contained deletions (ACDs). ACDs turn out to be an indicator for the presuppositional reading of an NP in that ACDs are only grammatical with presuppositional object NPs.

I also examine "specificity" in Dutch and Turkish and conclude that the "specific" indefinites in these languages correspond to the presuppositional, or box-splitting, reading of the indefinite. The Turkish data, which involve a relationship between morphological case marking and the presuppositional (QR) reading of an NP, raise the possibility of there being S-structure syntactic "triggers" (such as a case marker) for LF raising of an NP.

In chapter 4 I look more closely at the consequences of the nonuniform interpretation of indefinites. The focus of this chapter is on extraction from "picture" NPs. The acceptability of extraction from NP is rather controversial, and judgments on the data are notoriously fragile in that they "shift" very easily, depending on the context. I show that the possibility of extraction is closely linked to the availability of a nonpresuppositional reading for the NP. Extraction is prohibited from presuppositional NPs. This close link to presuppositionality explains the "shiftiness" in judgments, since the presuppositional nature of an NP depends in part on context.

The syntactic issue of "locality constraints" on extraction becomes an additional concern in chapter 4. The link between nonextractability and presupposition raises questions about the traditional means of accounting for extraction islands (Ross 1967). I show that the standard derivational approach to extraction from NP as an *S-structure* constraint against movement across a certain number of "bounding nodes" or barriers (Subjacency; see Chomsky 1977, 1986a), or as a constraint against movement out of an ungoverned domain (such as the Condition on Extraction Domain posited by Huang (1982)), is not adequate to account for the effects of presupposition on extractability.[6] I show that the relevant constraint must be stated in terms that take into account the *LF structure* of the sentence.

In contrast to chapter 2, which focuses on the interpretation of *subject* NPs, the emphasis in this chapter is on the interpretation of *object* NPs and the syntactic effects that follow from a particular interpretation. Given the workings of the Mapping Hypothesis and the results of chapter 3 concerning the syntactic differences between presuppositional and nonpresuppositional NPs, the presuppositional interpretation of object NPs in English requires that the NP be raised out of the VP by the rule of QR. The varying interpretations of object NPs are analyzed, taking into consideration the contexts in which they appear. I examine a number of different verb types and conclude that they differ with regard to which reading of an indefinite object, presuppositional or nonpresuppositional, they prefer.

Alongside the English data, I present German data involving S-structure "scrambling" of indefinite objects. I show that the semantic and syntactic effects of German scrambling parallel the effects of LF QR in English in that scrambling of an indefinite object results in the restrictive clause interpretation of the indefinite. Thus, scrambling appears to act as "S-structure QR" in these cases. This again raises the possibility that there may be S-structure triggers for QR, just as in the case of Turkish morphological case marking examined in chapter 3.

Finally, a few remarks are in order on the place of the Mapping Hypothesis within the overall picture of "semantic partition." Although I do not devote any attention to the more traditional forms of partitioning the sentence on semantic and/or pragmatic grounds, it is not my intention to suggest that the syntactic approach I take here should supplant notions such as topic/comment, theme/rheme, and subject/predicate. These sentential divisions encode various semantic and pragmatic distinctions that fall outside the range of phenomena to be discussed here. Thus, the Mapping Hypothesis is simply an additional source of partitioning, which will be shown to be amply justified in its own domain.

Chapter 2

Initial Evidence in Favor of
the Mapping Hypothesis

2.1 Introduction

The basic aim of this chapter is to provide specific empirical motivation
for the relationship between syntactic and logical representations proposed in the previous chapter in the form of a "tree-splitting algorithm,"
or Mapping Hypothesis:

(1) *Mapping Hypothesis*
    Material from VP is mapped into the nuclear scope.
    Material from IP is mapped into a restrictive clause.

The procedure in (1) not only outlines the derivation of logical representations, but also makes a number of predictions concerning interactions
between syntactic phenomena and the semantics of NPs. I present here a
variety of data that support the notion that there is such a correspondence
between the syntactic and logical representations.

   Since the subject/nonsubject contrast is pivotal in the VP/IP distinction
emphasized in (1), I first concentrate on the interpretation of indefinite
subjects. My initial claim is that different predicate types show different
properties with respect to the possible interpretations of subjects and their
distribution, and these contrasts can be easily accounted for by the procedure in (1). As a starting point I introduce a particular distinction of
predicate types that highlights the "splitting" of the sentence effected by
the Mapping Hypothesis in a number of different ways. This classification
is the *stage/individual* distinction of Carlson (1977b). Various syntactic
and semantic properties of the subjects of these two predicate types provide support for the hypothesis in (1). In the final sections of this chapter
I extend my approach to a number of other predicate types.

2.2   The Readings of Bare Plurals

In and of itself, the form of the logical representations introduced in
the previous chapter makes certain predictions concerning the interpretation of subjects. The tree-splitting diagram (along with the representa-
tion(s) derived by the procedure) implies that there are two possible positions for the subject in the logical representation. A subject in [Spec, IP]
will map into a restrictive clause, and a subject in [Spec, VP] will map into
the nuclear scope. The first thing to consider in investigating the empirical
validity of the Mapping Hypothesis is whether or not these two possibilities are actually both attested in the interpretations of subjects. In this
section I focus on a particular class of NP, the English bare plural, and
consider the two possibilities for representing the interpretations of these
subjects in the logical representations. I conclude that we do in fact need
both positions for the subject in the semantic representation.

Bare plurals are a particular kind of indefinite NP that do not have an
overt determiner of any kind. As observed by Carlson (1977b), English
bare plural subjects can receive either a generic or an existential reading:

(2) a. Brussels sprouts are unsuitable for eating.
  b. Carpenter ants destroyed my viola da gamba.

The example in (2a) illustrates the generic reading. (2a) is not a statement
about any particular Brussels sprouts. Instead, it states that *in general*
Brussels sprouts have the property of not being edible. The bare plural
subject in (2b), on the other hand, exemplifies the existential reading. This
is not a statement about a property of carpenter ants in general; it merely
asserts the existence of some carpenter ants that ate my viola da gamba.

In deriving the logical representations of these two readings, I will
assume (following Wilkinson (1986) and Gerstner and Krifka (1987)) that
there is an abstract generic operator *Gen* that binds variables to produce a
generic reading. I will also assume that bare plurals, like certain singular
indefinites such as *a llama*, introduce variables into the logical representation. Thus, the two readings of the bare plural subject in (2) result from
different representations in Heim's framework:[1]

(3) a. Gen_x [x is a Brussels sprout] x is unsuitable for eating
  b. $\exists_x$ x is a carpenter ant $\wedge$ x destroyed my viola da gamba

In (3a) the bare plural NP *Brussels sprouts* is introduced in the restrictive
clause and is bound by the operator *Gen*, which gives the generic reading—
in general, those things that are Brussels sprouts are unsuitable for eating.

In (3b) the NP *carpenter ants* appears in the nuclear scope and is bound by existential closure, resulting in the existential reading—there were some carpenter ants that destroyed my viola da gamba.

Carlson notes, however, that not all predicates allow both the generic and existential readings for a bare plural subject. Carlson distinguishes two types of predicates, *stage-level* predicates and *individual-level* predicates. Stage-level predicates typically correspond to temporary states such as "available" and "lying on the floor" and transitory activities such as "destroying my viola da gamba" and "falling down the stairs." Individual-level predicates roughly correspond to more or less permanent states such as "unsuitable for eating," "intelligent," and "having six legs."[2] In the following sections I examine more closely the behavior of these two types of predicates. After considering the distribution of readings for bare plural subjects, I show that the two kinds of predicates differ in where they allow a bare plural subject to appear in the logical representation, providing the first step in justifying the Mapping Hypothesis.

In particular, I discuss the different possible readings of bare plural subjects with stage-level and individual-level adjectival predicates. The distribution of the readings possible with the two types of predicates leads to a formulation of the stage/individual contrast in terms of where the subject NPs of each type of predicate can be represented in the logical representations.

2.2.1 Stage-Level Predicates

Close examination of sentences with stage-level predicates reveals that not only are both existential and generic quantification allowed, but there are also apparent interactions between existential quantification and generic quantification. In other words, a stage-level predicate can induce both existential properties and generic properties at the same time. Thus, a stage-level predicate like *available* allows the following readings:

(4) a. Firemen are available.
   b. $\exists_x$ x is a fireman $\wedge$ x is available
   c. Gen$_{x,t}$ [x is a fireman $\wedge$ t is a time] x is available at t
   d. Gen$_t$ [t is a time] $\exists_x$ x is a fireman $\wedge$ x is available at t

The first reading given in (4) is the existential reading of the bare plural subject. On this reading there are firemen available at some point in time. This reading involves an "episodic" reading of the predicate, along with an existential reading of the subject.

The second reading is a generic reading expressing a dispositional attribute of firemen; it is a necessary property of firemen that they be generally available for fighting fires. It follows from this reading that a person who is likely to give other commitments a higher priority than firefighting shouldn't be a fireman. Unlike (4b), this reading is not episodic, but involves some sort of generic tense (see Carlson 1977b) as a result of the generic operator binding times as well as firemen (as shown in the restrictive clause in (4c)).

Finally, in the third reading the existential quantification is under the scope of a generic operator, producing an "existential generic" interpretation. This reading can be paraphrased as 'Generally, there are firemen available'. In this case the generic operator may perhaps bind times, as shown in (4d). One context in which this reading may arise is the situation where firemen work short shifts, but there are always some firemen on call. Thus, not only can the stage-level adjectival predicates induce both generic and existential readings for bare plural subjects, but they are also ambiguous between episodic and generic tense so that multiple generic readings are in fact possible as a result of the interaction of the generic operator with existential closure.[3] In what follows in this chapter I will concentrate mainly on the occurrence or nonoccurrence of the existential and generic readings, without discussing the interactions between the various readings any further.

2.2.2 Individual-Level Predicates

Whereas bare plural subjects of stage-level predicates receive either the existential or the generic interpretation, bare plural subjects of individual-level predicates appear to be more restricted. There is a striking asymmetry between the two types of predicates with respect to subject interpretation. Individual-level adjectival predicates seem to allow only the generic reading of their bare plural subjects, and do not seem to allow existential readings at all. This is illustrated in (5).

(5) a. Violists are intelligent.
     b. Opera singers know Italian.

Consideration of the examples in (5) reveals that the absence of the existential reading cannot be attributed to pragmatic factors (unlike the case of the sometimes implausible generic readings with stage-level predicates; see note 3). The lack of an existential reading in (5a) has nothing to do with whether or not the subject NP *violists* can be appropriately applied to *intelligent*. It is difficult, if not impossible, to think of any contextual situations in which (5a) could be taken to mean 'There are intelligent violists'. The same observation applies to the predicate *know Italian* in (5b) with respect to the subject *opera singers*. Thus, stage- and individual-level predicates differ in the interpretive possibilities they allow for bare plural subjects. Whereas bare plural subjects of stage-level predicates can be bound by either the generic operator *Gen* or existential closure (or of course an overt adverb of quantification such as *always*), subjects of individual-level predicates can only be bound by the generic operator (or an adverb of quantification). Since the *Gen* operator only binds variables that are introduced in the restrictive clause of the logical representation, this difference between the two types of predicates can be expressed in terms of a difference in where the subject NPs can appear in the logical representation:

(6) *Stage-Individual-level distinction*
     In a logical representation, bare plural subjects of stage-level
     predicates can appear in either the nuclear scope (to be bound by
     existential closure) or the restrictive clause (to be bound by either the
     abstract quantifier *Gen* or an overt operator). Bare plural subjects of
     individual-level predicates can only appear in the restrictive clause.[4]

Thus, a bare plural subject can be mapped into either of the two possible positions in the logical representation, either the nuclear scope or the restrictive clause. The data concerning the multiple interpretations of the English bare plural show that we do indeed need both positions for the subject in the logical representation. At this point, the generalization stated in (6) is merely descriptive. There still remain the questions of how the mapping from the syntax to the logical representations is accomplished, and of why the two types of predicates should be distinguished in this way. In the next section I propose how the two types of subjects may be distinguished in the syntax to make the mapping to logical representations possible. This in turn leads to proposing a syntactic distinction between stage- and individual-level predicates that derives the distinction in (6).

2.3   The Syntactic Connection: Deriving the Two Readings

The Mapping Hypothesis under consideration here maintains that there is a correspondence between the two subject positions in the syntactic tree and the two possible positions for the subject in the logical representations illustrated in (3). In this section I examine the relationship between the tree-splitting process and restrictive clause formation, or box splitting, by taking a closer look at the syntactic derivations of the two readings of the bare plural subject.

I will concentrate on the basic existential and generic readings of the sentence *Firemen are available* shown in (4b) and (4c), beginning with the existential reading.

(7) *Deriving the existential reading*

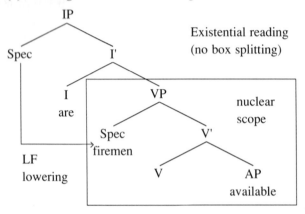

The tree in (7) shows the derivation of the existential reading of (4). The subject lowers from its S-structure position in [Spec, IP] to the VP-internal subject position [Spec, VP] (I will discuss the question of where the subject is base-generated later on).[5] This is similar to the quantifier lowering operation proposed by May (1977, 1985) to account for scope ambiguities in raising constructions. This entails that there is some abstract syntactic level of "logical form" (which I will call *LF*, following May (1977) and others) intervening between S-structure and the level of semantic representation. I will assume, just as in the quantifier-lowering case discussed by May, that the trace left by the lowered NP is interpreted as an empty expletive at LF and thus need not be bound at LF (see May 1985:102).[6] Tree splitting then applies (at the abstract level of LF), mapping the VP into the nuclear scope. The IP-level subtree is left empty, and therefore no restrictive clause is formed (or, following the parallel to Kamp's (1981) box-splitting operation, tree splitting produces only one box). This leads to the representation in (4b).[7]

In deriving the generic reading, on the other hand, no LF lowering of the bare plural subject takes place. The subject stays in [Spec, IP], where it is mapped into a restrictive clause by the mapping algorithm. From this LF configuration, tree splitting produces two boxes: a restrictive clause and a nuclear scope. The variable introduced in the restrictive clause is bound by the generic operator. Since no new variables are introduced in the VP in this case, existential closure does not apply. This is shown in (8), which corresponds to the logical representation in (4c).

(8) *Deriving the generic reading*

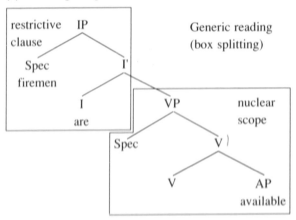

The syntactic derivation of the generic and existential readings of (4) raises a question about the levels of representation involved: namely, When in the derivation of a sentence does the mapping to logical representations (tree splitting) occur? In English, it is clear that it cannot be at S-structure, since all subjects must appear in [Spec, IP] at S-structure. There is no way to distinguish IP subjects (in [Spec, IP]) and VP subjects (in [Spec, VP]) at S-structure in English. The mapping to logical representations must therefore occur at the intermediate syntactic level of LF (see May 1977, 1985). The generic and existential readings are distinguished by the fact that LF lowering of the subject to the VP-internal subject position occurs in the existential reading but not in the generic reading. To return to the question of the relation between the syntactic representations and the semantic representations, given these assumptions about the derivation of logical representations, there is in fact a correspondence (albeit an indirect one mediated by the level of LF) between the two subject positions in the logical representations and the two subject positions in the phrase structure tree.

Only stage-level predicates permit both the derivations in (7) and (8). With individual-level predicates only the generic reading (illustrated by the derivation in (8)) is possible. Thus, at the point of mapping to logical representations (e.g., the level of LF) the bare plural subject of an individual-level predicate must be in [Spec, IP], in order to be mapped into a restrictive clause, where it will be bound by the generic operator. The distinction between stage- and individual-level predicates stated in (6) can be restated in terms of the possible syntactic position of the bare plural subject at the level of LF:

(9) *LF representation of bare plural subjects*
    Subjects of stage-level predicates can appear either in [Spec, IP] or in [Spec, VP]. Subjects of individual-level predicates can appear only in [Spec, IP].

Although this translation into syntactic terms addresses the question of how the two readings are derived, it still leaves open the question of why the two predicate types should differ in just this way. From the derivations in (7) and (8) it might be expected that subjects of individual-level predicates such as *intelligent* should have the option of lowering the subject to [Spec, VP] at LF, just as in the case of the stage-level predicate *available*. Nothing in the analysis as presented so far precludes this possibility.

Kratzer (1989) proposes to derive the difference from a difference in argument structure. She proposes that stage-level predicates have an abstract "Davidsonian" spatiotemporal external argument, whereas individual-level predicates lack this argument.[8] She gives various kinds of evidence for the existence of the abstract spatiotemporal argument in stage-level predicates, including availability of the spatiotemporal argument for binding as a variable by an operator. This difference in argument structure is used to derive the syntactic difference between the two types of predicates stated in (9) through argument-linking conventions. Taking the argument-linking analysis of Williams (1981) as a starting point, Kratzer assumes that all arguments except the external argument are realized at D-structure within the maximal projection of their predicate (the VP in this case). The external argument (if not implicit, as in the case of the abstract Davidsonian argument) then appears external to the predicate (in [Spec, IP]).

Thus, in Kratzer's account the difference between stage- and individual-level predicates is due to a difference in argument structure. In particular, the two predicate types differ in their external arguments: stage-level predicates have the abstract Davidsonian argument, whereas individual-level predicates (or, more accurately, individual-level predicates that have an external argument) map the subject NP to the external position at D-structure. In the case of the individual-level predicates the subjects are base-generated in [Spec, IP], and subjects of stage-level predicates are base-generated in [Spec, VP].

2.3.1 Control, Raising, and the Stage/Individual Contrast

The argument-linking approach taken by Kratzer unifies the explanation of the variable-binding properties of the two types of predicates with the explanation of the other semantic properties of the predicates (e.g., the possible interpretations of bare plural subjects). This unification is accomplished at the cost of making some unorthodox assumptions about argument linking. In any case, it is no longer clear that the external argument must be base-generated external to VP (as proposed by Williams), since the VP-Internal Subject Hypothesis permits θ-marking of the external argument within VP (see Kitagawa 1986 and also Larson 1988 for some proposals in which all arguments are projected from base positions within VP).

Kratzer's proposal also rules out the possibility of there being *any* connection between the external subject and the internal subject position ([Spec, VP]) in individual-level predicates. There is some preliminary evidence that this restriction may not be correct. Bonet (1989), citing data from Catalan, suggests that floated quantifier constructions might require that all subjects be base-generated in [Spec, VP]. Her claim is based on the fact that floated-quantifier constructions are acceptable with individual-level predicates (incidentally, this is true of English as well). The logic of Bonet's argument follows the NP-movement analysis of floated quantifiers proposed by Sportiche (1988) in which the floated quantifier originates from the internal (or lower) subject position. Thus, on Sportiche's analysis the subject in the following sentence has raised from a position adjacent to the floated quantifier *all* (the subject NP is base-generated as *all the violists*):

(10) a. [$_{IP}$ The violists$_i$ are [$_{VP}$ all t$_i$ tone-deaf]].

If the subject were base-generated in [Spec, IP] with no connection to [Spec,VP], this relation between the S-structure subject and the floated quantifier could not hold.

The sentence in (10) makes it clear that it must be possible for the subject of an individual-level predicate to be related to the lower position in some way, regardless of whether or not floated-quantifier constructions involve an actual *movement* relation, rather than some other sort of relation between the two subject positions. I would like to propose a variation

on Kratzer's approach that is consistent with the results of Bonet and
Sportiche in that it permits an "anaphoric" relationship of some kind to
exist between the two subject positions with both types of predicates,
although the nature of the relation differs in each case.

My claim is that the difference between the two types of predicates arises
from differences in the properties of the Infl associated with them. As
shown in (11), stage-level predicates have an "unaccusative" (in the sense
of having an internal subject) Infl: the subject is base-generated internal to
the VP in [Spec, VP], and Infl does not assign a θ-role to [Spec, IP].
This gives rise to a "raising" relation between the two subject positions.

(11) *Stage-level predicate*

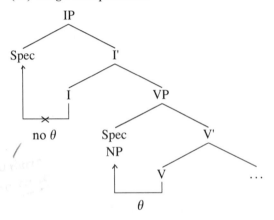

The pattern of θ-assignment illustrated in (11) permits S-structure raising of the subject of a stage-level predicate to [Spec, IP] to receive case,
leaving a trace in [Spec, VP], analogous to raising predicates. The raising
analogy also applies to the "LF lowering" operation used to derive the
existential reading of the subject. As mentioned earlier, May (1977, 1985)
shows that subjects of raising predicates can be interpreted as though they
have been lowered at LF, in an "undoing" of NP-movement. In parallel
to raising predicates, stage-level predicates also allow lowering of the
subject from [Spec, IP] into the lower subject position, [Spec, VP], in the
mapping to LF.

Thus, subjects of stage-level predicates at LF may stay in [Spec, IP], or
they may be lowered to their base position in [Spec, VP]. Stage-level
predicates can thus receive either a generic interpretation (subject remains
in [Spec, IP] at LF) or an existential interpretation (subject is lowered into
[Spec, VP] at LF). Subjects of raising predicates like *seem* also can be
interpreted as if lowered at LF. Thus, in the sentence in (12) the indefinite

NP *a unicorn* may be interpreted as having either wide or narrow scope with respect to the matrix predicate.

(12) A unicorn is likely to damage the walls.

Empirical support for this "lowering" analysis of the bare plural subject of stage-level predicates comes from binding facts in multiple raising structures, or sentences in which a stage-level predicate is embedded as the complement of a raising verb.[9]

(13) a. Firemen$_i$ seem to their$_i$ employers to be available.
    b. Gila monsters$_i$ seem to their$_i$ predators to be visible.

In the sentences in (13) the bare plural subjects *firemen* and *Gila monsters* show a dependency between the generic reading and the pronominal binding shown in the indexing given. The bound variable relation between the bare plural and the pronoun forces the generic reading. The sentence in (13a) cannot mean 'There are firemen that seem to their employers to be available'. If the existential reading is derived by lowering of the subject as proposed above, the absence of this reading in the sentences in (13) is actually expected. Lowering of the subject into the lower VP would rule out the bound variable reading for the pronoun *their* since the subject would no longer c-command the pronoun (assuming that these binding relationships must hold at LF):

(14) e$_i$ seem to their$_i$ employers [to be [firemen$_i$ available]]

This contrasts with parallel sentences without a bound pronoun, in which both the "lowered" (existential) and "raised" (generic) readings of the bare plural are possible (although the sentences are somewhat awkward):

(15) a. Firemen seem to the mayor to be available.
    b. Gila monsters seem to the coyotes to be visible.

Thus, the absence of the existential reading on the bound variable interpretation of the pronoun in (13) supports the lowering analysis of the derivation of the existential reading.

The raising analysis of stage-level predicates accounts for the fact that they permit both the generic and existential readings of bare plural subjects. This leaves us with the matter of accounting for why individual-level subjects are restricted to the generic reading. My proposal here is that individual-level predicates should be analyzed as analogues to control predicates. On this account, as illustrated in (16), individual-level predicates differ from stage-level predicates in that they have an Infl that assigns a θ-role to [Spec, IP]. This role has roughly the meaning 'has the property x', where x is the property expressed by the predicate. The lexical NP in [Spec, IP] controls a PRO subject in [Spec, VP], which is assigned a θ-role by the verb.

(16) *Individual-level predicate*

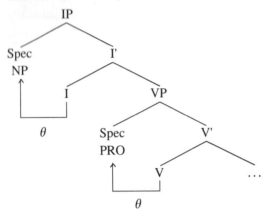

The "control Infl" is thus a two-place predicate, with the subject NP and the VP as arguments.

The presence of PRO in [Spec, VP] raises the question of the government status of the [Spec, VP] position. As required by the PRO Theorem (see Chomsky 1981 and related works), PRO must be ungoverned. In the configuration in (16), the PRO in [Spec, VP] is θ-marked by V, and presumably also governed by it (we will see empirical evidence for the assumption that [Spec, VP] is a governed position later on in this chapter).[10] If PRO were to remain in this position, the proposal would be inconsistent with the assumptions that led to the formulation of the PRO Theorem.

There are a couple of ways of dealing with this problem. One could simply propose that contrary to Chomsky (1981), PRO may be governed in English. There are in fact a number of analyses of various phenomena that independently support the notion of a governed PRO; see, for example, Haider 1983, É. Kiss 1987, Koster 1987, and Sigurðsson 1990.

Alternatively, one could choose to maintain the PRO Theorem and assume that the PRO in [Spec, VP] in (16) is simply forced to move to an ungoverned position external to VP, a position that might not otherwise be generated. Here again there is evidence that a mechanism of this kind is independently necessary. In order to maintain the idea that PRO must be ungoverned, forced movement of PRO out of a governed position is necessary in contexts involving control into passives:

(17) Hector tried to be killed.

One possible candidate for the landing site for the moved PRO would be the specifier of Pesetsky's (1989) μ-phrase (the μ-phrase is used by Pesetsky as a sort of all-purpose escape hatch). Thus, on this approach PRO may be generated in a governed position, but it must not remain there throughout the derivation. I will not choose between these two options for dealing with the problem of a governed PRO, but will simply leave the matter for further research.

The parallel to control predicates also shows up in the available semantic interpretations of the bare plural subjects of individual-level predicates. As noted by May (1985), the subjects of control predicates such as *be anxious to* do not lower in the mapping to LF, since the [Spec, IP] is assigned a θ-role. Thus, the subject of a control predicate can only have wide scope with respect to the matrix predicate:

(18) A unicorn is anxious to damage the walls.

Likewise, subjects of individual-level predicates are not able to lower and therefore *must* be mapped into the restrictive clause at LF, receiving only the generic reading:

(19) a. [$_{IP}$ Opera singers [$_{VP}$ PRO know Italian]].
    b. Gen$_x$ [x is an opera singer] x knows Italian

Thus, the fact that only the generic reading is possible with individual-level predicates can be accounted for by the fact that subjects of individual-level predicates are base-generated in [Spec, IP]. They have not undergone NP-movement, raising them from [Spec, VP], and thus cannot be lowered. Thus, the only possible position for the subject of an individual-level predicate at LF is the outer subject position, or the position corresponding to the restrictive clause.

If the distinctions in behavior between the two types of predicates are due to a difference in Infl, the question arises how this difference is to be represented in the case of *adjectival* predicates. Following Stump (1985), I will assume that there are (at least) two verbs *be*. The first is a predicative *be* that selects an individual-level adjective and forms an individual-level predicate (Stump's *be$_2$*, p. 75). The second *be* selects a stage-level adjective to form a stage-level predicate (Stump's *be$_4$*, p. 79).[11] The individual-level *be* takes the individual-level Infl, and the stage-level *be* takes the stage-level Infl.[12] I will return to the question of classifying adjectives according to the stage/individual distinction in a later section. This alternation between two types of *be* is perhaps comparable to the alternation between the *be*-forms *ser* and *estar* in Spanish.[13]

Summarizing this section, I have proposed to analyze the stage/individual contrast as being analogous to the contrast between raising and control predicates. This sort of analysis parallels descriptions of epistemic modals as raising verbs (see Jackendoff 1972, McCawley 1988:211–213), as opposed to root modals, which may involve a control-like structure (Zubizarreta 1982).[14] The contrast centers on a difference in Infl: individual-level predicates take the "control" Infl that assigns a θ-role to [Spec, IP], which has roughly the meaning 'has the property *x*'. The subject is thus base-generated in [Spec, IP], but controls a PRO subject in the VP-internal subject position. Stage-level predicates, on the other hand, take an Infl that does not assign this θ-role to [Spec, IP].[15] In this case the subject is base-generated in [Spec, VP] and raises to [Spec, IP] at S-structure. Stage- and individual-level predicates are further distinguished with respect to the presence or absence of an event argument. These two properties are shown in (20):

(20) *Properties of stage- and individual-level predicates*

	Stage	Individual
θ-role to [Spec, IP]?	no	yes
Event argument?	yes	no

My account differs from Kratzer's (1989) analysis in that the subject of an individual-level predicate in [Spec, IP] still bears a control relationship to the internal [Spec, VP] position. This is desirable, because it is consistent with the fact that floated quantifiers do not show a stage- and individual-level contrast, as pointed out by Bonet (1989). The control analysis of individual-level predicates allows the needed connection between the subject NP and the VP in the floated-quantifier construction, since (as noted by Sportiche (1988)) floated quantifiers can to some extent "originate" from PRO in the "usual" control structures:

(21) The violists promised to all leave.

Thus, the lexical NP associated with the floated quantifier need not be base-generated in the internal position to allow floated quantifiers with individual-level predicates.

The classification given in (20) leads one to wonder about other possible settings of the two parameters shown there: θ-role assignment to the external subject position and the presence of the event argument. One possibility relates to a particular class of predicates discussed by Kratzer

(1989) (although the discussion does not occur in this connection). This case is what Kratzer refers to as "individual-level unaccusatives." These amount to predicates that lack an event argument and allow the surface subject to be generated VP-internally as an underlying object. No θ-role is assigned to [Spec, IP]. Thus, on Kratzer's analysis these predicates are those that do not assign a θ-role to an external subject, and also do not have an event argument. Examples are verbs like *belong to* and *is known to*:

(22) a. Snow leopards belong to the emperor.

b. Counterexamples are known to most linguists.

Though the sentences in (22) do have a "universal flavor" of sorts, they do not seem to express generic qualities of their subjects (snow leopards and counterexamples). If anything, they express properties of their objects (the emperor and linguists).

I would like to suggest that the universal nature of these sentences derives from binding by the generic operator *Gen*, whereas the absence of the 'has property x' reading results from the fact that no θ-role is assigned to [Spec, IP]. However, it is important to note that as Kratzer has argued, these predicates differ from stage-level predicates in that they give no evidence of having an event argument. I will discuss the properties of the individual-level unaccusatives in more detail in a later section.

2.3.2 Existential Closure and Bare Plural Objects

One final point to note is that this account predicts that there should be no generic readings for bare plural objects. This is because existential closure applies to VPs, binding all variables within VP. VP-internal bare plurals should therefore receive only the existential interpretation. In most cases, genericity does indeed appear to be subject-oriented. This fact is discussed by Carlson (1977b).

The observation that generic interpretations are limited to subjects does not hold generally for all types of predicates, however. Carlson (1977: 186ff.) notes that there are some transitive verbs that do result in generic readings for bare plural objects. These are verbs such as *like, hate, fear,* and *loathe*—the so-called experiencer predicates:

(23) a. Cellists hate boring bass lines.

b. Contrabassoonists love chocolate chip cookies.

In the sentences in (23) both the subject and object seem to be interpreted generically.[16] Thus, it appears that objects of experiencer predicates can somehow "escape" the nuclear scope and be mapped into the restrictive clause, to be bound by *Gen* along with the subject. Some light can be shed on this situation by considering free word order, or "scrambling," in German. Kratzer (1989) notes that there is a parallel between these cases and S-structure scrambling of indefinites in German in that whereas indefinites are normally barred from scrambling out of VP in German (Lenerz 1977), indefinite objects of experiencer verbs generally do scramble. Kratzer therefore proposes that objects of experiencer predicates in English are scrambled out of the VP at LF (presumably adjoining to IP) and can thus be mapped into the restrictive clause.

The generic reading for an object bare plural is not strictly limited to the objects of experiencer verbs (although experiencer verbs are special in that they *require* generic readings for bare plural objects). In certain "habitual" contexts other verb types permit generic readings for bare plural objects as well. In (24) the bare plural NP *novels* can receive a generic interpretation in a context where whenever Esther comes upon a novel, she reads it.

(24) Esther reads novels.

Interestingly, contexts such as that given for (24) also permit scrambling of indefinites in the parallel sentences in German (see also Kratzer 1989 and Kathol 1989). I will therefore assume that these cases in English also involve LF scrambling of the object NP, which subsequently results in the object NP being mapped into a restrictive clause. (I will discuss constructions of this type in both English and German in detail in chapter 4.)

2.3.3 Overview of Stage- and Individual-Level Predicates

The interpretations of bare plural subjects reflect a correspondence between the X-bar syntactic representation at LF and the Heim-style logical representations in which the VP maps into the nuclear scope and material outside of the VP maps into the restrictive clause.[17] The interpretive differences between subjects of stage- and individual-level predicates are thus due to a syntactic contrast. Whereas all subjects appear in [Spec, IP] at S-structure in English, at LF the subjects of stage- and individual-level predicates differ in position: individual-level subjects can only appear in the outer position and are mapped into the restrictive clause, whereas stage-level subjects can appear in the inner position and be mapped into the nuclear scope. This difference derives from differing properties of Infl in the two types of predicates, which results in the stage-level predicates being given an analysis parallel to raising verbs, and individual-level predicates being analyzed as parallel to control structures.

In this section I have confirmed the first prediction made by the Mapping Hypothesis: the existence of two possible positions for the subject in the logical representation is motivated by the English bare plural facts. In demonstrating this, I noted that the relationship between S-structure and the logical representations in English is necessarily somewhat abstract, since in English all subjects must appear in [Spec, IP] at S-structure. In the next section I consider the possibility of a more direct relationship between the restrictive clause/nuclear scope positions and the syntactic [Spec, IP]/[Spec, VP] positions, in order to confirm the close relation between the syntactic tree and the logical representations that is imposed by the tree-splitting algorithm. This requires focusing on a language in which subjects need not appear in [Spec, IP] at S-structure. One language where this seems to be the case is German.

2.4 Two Subject Positions in German: An IP/VP Contrast

German provides data that permit the possibility of a more direct relationship between the tree-splitting procedure and the S-structure representations than that described for English in the previous section. In German it appears that it is not necessary for the subject to appear in [Spec, IP] at S-structure. Thus, in the sentences in (25) the subject NP *Ameisen* 'ants' can appear either to the left or to the right of the sentential particles *ja* and *doch*.[18] As we will see, this freedom of word order provides a basis for testing the relationship between the syntactic structure and the semantic interpretation of a sentence.

(25) a. ... [CP weil [IP Ameisen ja doch [VP einen Postbeamten gebissen
                since   ants   'indeed'   a   postman   bitten
     haben]]].
     have
   b. ... [CP weil [IP ja doch [VP Ameisen einen Postbeamten gebissen
                since 'indeed'   ants   a   postman   bitten
     haben]]].
     have

I have bracketed the sentences in (25) in such a way as to indicate that the subject to the left of the particles (as in (25a)) is immediately dominated by the IP node and the subject to the right of the particles (as in (25b)) is immediately dominated by the VP node. It has in fact been argued by Jackendoff (1972) for English, by Holmberg (1986) for Scandinavian, and by Webelhuth (1989) for German that sentence adverbials mark the VP boundary. Arguments involving relative positioning of elements have also been used by Pollock (1989) to argue for phrase structure positions (inflectional heads in particular) in an articulated inflectional structure. This is not the strongest sort of evidence to use in investigating clause structure, however. It may be possible that the "reference points" (in this instance the adverbials) themselves may move by some process (such as scrambling). Therefore, before considering the semantic implications of the two possible word orders in (25), it is worthwhile to seek additional evidence going beyond arguments based on relative position to support the claim that the two apparent subject positions shown are in fact the [Spec, IP] or [Spec, VP] positions. To this end, I consider two cases of extraction in German that show a contrast in acceptability depending on the apparent S-structure position of the subject.

2.4.1 Extraction and the Two Subject Positions

The first case of extraction I will consider is the *was-für* split, The *was-für* split is a case of extraction out of NPs (subextraction) discussed by Den Besten (1985) (the Dutch counterpart of this construction, the *wat-voor* split, is also discussed by Bennis (1986)). The NP specifier *was-für* (meaning 'what kind of') can occur as a lexical unit, or the *was* portion can break off and be fronted to [Spec, CP] by *wh*-movement, leaving the rest of the NP behind:

(26) a. Was für Ameisen haben denn   einen Postbeamten gebissen?
         what for ants   have 'indeed' a   postman   bitten
         'What kind of ants have bitten a postman?'

   b. [$_{CP}$ Was haben [$_{IP}$ denn [$_{VP}$ für Ameisen einen Postbeamten
         ↑_____|

       gebissen]]]?

   c. *[$_{CP}$ Was haben [$_{IP}$ für Ameisen denn [$_{VP}$ einen Postbeamten
         ↑_____|

       gebissen]]]?

In (26a) the entire subject NP *was für Ameisen* has been fronted to [Spec, CP] by *wh*-movement. No splitting of the specifier *was-für* has taken place. In (26b) only the *was* portion of the specifier has been fronted, leaving the remainder of the NP behind to the right of the particle *denn* (the arrow indicates the movement that has taken place). (26c) illustrates the case in which *was* is extracted out of a subject that is to the *left* of the sentential particle, as indicated by the "stranded" portion of the NP. In this case the extraction is not acceptable. Den Besten (1985) has argued that the *was-für* split is indeed a case of movement, on the basis that it is possible only from "governed positions."

A second case of movement in German that shows a contrast between the two subject positions is the *split-topic* construction. This construction has been the subject of much recent work (see, for example, Van Riemsdijk 1989, Fanselow 1988a, Tappe 1989, and Bhatt 1990). I will simply assume here that just as in the *was-für* split, extraction (e.g., topicalization) from an NP has taken place, with the result that a portion of the NP has been fronted to the "topic" position preceding the finite verb and a determiner is left stranded in the base position (for specific arguments that this construction does indeed show properties characteristic of movement, see Van Riemsdijk 1989).[19] This construction raises a number of interesting problems, many of which are discussed in the references mentioned. I will be focusing in particular on extraction from subjects, as in (27).

(27) a. Ameisen$_i$ haben ja   einen Postbeamten [$_{NP}$ viele t$_i$] gebissen.

   ants   have PRT a   postman   many   bitten
   'As for ants, many have bitten a postman.'
 b. *Ameisen haben viele ja   einen Postbeamten gebissen.
   ants   have many PRT a   postman   bitten

As illustrated here, the split-topic construction shows the same contrast with respect to extractability from a subject as the *was-für* split. Subjects in an internal position (to the right of the sentential particle *ja*) permit subextraction (27a), whereas subjects in the external position (to the left of the particle) do not allow extraction (27b).

Thus, the relative position of the subject determines extractability in both the *was-für* split and split-topic constructions. The original observations of Den Besten (1985) and Van Riemsdijk (1989) concerned the contrast between extraction from subjects of unaccusatives and extraction from unergatives. They did not note the distinction between internal and external subjects in unergatives shown above (this distinction was originally noted by Angelika Kratzer in class lectures in the spring of 1988).

These contrasts in extraction provide evidence concerning the relative structural position of the two subject positions. If the two subject positions (to the left and the right of the sentential particles) are structurally distinguished as [Spec, IP] and [Spec, VP], Kratzer's observations concerning extraction can be assimilated to Huang's (1982) discussion of the restriction against extraction from subjects (a subcase of his Condition on Extraction Domain, or CED). In this case the position to which the

CED-like constraint applies is the [Spec, IP], as opposed to [Spec, VP], which carries no restriction on extraction.

Huang's results have been reanalyzed in terms of Subjacency violations in the *Barriers* framework of Chomsky (1986a). I will adopt Chomsky's analysis to show that the extraction contrast between (26b)/(26c) and (27a)/(27b) can be explained as a Subjacency contrast *if* the leftmost subject position is assumed to be [Spec, IP] and the right-hand subject position is assumed to be [Spec, VP].

In the *Barriers* framework a Subjacency violation is defined as resulting from crossing two categories that are barriers to movement. The definition of a barrier is relational and involves the interplay of several different concepts. In (28)–(31) I give the relevant definitions from Chomsky 1986a.

(28) *Barrier*
γ is a barrier for β iff (a) or (b):
  a. γ immediately dominates δ, δ a blocking category (BC) for β;
  b. γ is a BC for β, $\gamma \neq$ IP.

(29) *Blocking category*
γ is a BC for β iff γ is not L-marked and γ dominates β.

(30) *L-marking*
α L-marks β iff α is a lexical category that θ-governs β. (α θ-marks β and is a sister to β)

(31) *Spec-head agreement*
If a head L-marks a maximal projection, it L-marks the specifier of the projection. (Koopman and Sportiche 1988)

This system can be applied to explain the contrasts in extraction noted above, but some minor revisions have to be made. The first modification arises in considering the cases of [Spec, VP] extraction in (26b) and (27a). Here the lexicalized Infl (V + Infl) L-marks VP (as Chomsky (1986a) assumes in discussing raising). I make an additional assumption, which is that aspectual verbs like *have* (or the German *haben*, in this case) L-mark their complements, just as other verbs do (this assumption is also made by Tappe (1989) with regard to the split-topic construction; see also Bhatt 1990 for further discussion).

Since the VP is L-marked, the [Spec, VP] is also L-marked, by means of Spec-head agreement, as defined in (31). In this case the L-marking head is the lexicalized Infl (or V + Infl), the maximal projection is the VP, and the specifier of VP ([Spec, VP]) is thereby L-marked. This is an extension of the original notion of Spec-head agreement as put forth by Chomsky

(1986a). Originally Spec-head agreement was proposed for cases where IP was L-marked (such as an embedded clause in exceptional case marking (ECM) contexts). The agreement mechanism was motivated by the case-assigning relationship between [Spec, IP] and Agr (Chomsky 1986a:24). Chomsky then extended this agreement relation to the head and specifier of CP (p. 27), characterizing the specifier-head relation in terms of the sharing of some abstract "ϕ-features." I simply extend this idea to heads and specifiers generally, as expressed in definition (31).[20]

The result is that in (26b) neither the VP nor [Spec, VP] is a blocking category, since by definition (29) a blocking category is necessarily *not* L-marked. A further consequence is that neither the VP nor [Spec, VP] is a barrier, since a barrier must either itself be a blocking category or immediately dominate a blocking category (see definition (28)). Thus, extraction out of a subject in [Spec, VP] does not cross any barriers and should therefore be good. This is what we see in (26b) and (27a).

In the case of (26c) and (27b), or the [Spec, IP] extractions, IP is *not* L-marked. There is subsequently no Spec-head agreement, and [Spec, IP] is therefore also not L-marked. Since it is not L-marked, [Spec, IP] is a blocking category (by definition (29)). [Spec, IP] is thereby also a barrier, by clause (b) of the definition of barrier in (28), since it is a blocking category and not equal to IP. The IP in turn then "inherits" barrierhood by clause (a) of the definition of barrier: it dominates [Spec, IP], which is a blocking category. Thus, extraction from the [Spec, IP] crosses *two* barriers, [Spec, IP] and IP, and the result is ungrammatical.

In summary, the position of the subject relative to sentential particles (either to the left or to the right) led to the observation that there are at least two positions for the subject in German. The contrasts in extractability between the two subject positions in the *was-für* split and the split-topic construction provide evidence that the two positions are distinguished in the *Barriers* framework with respect to Subjacency. In obtaining this result, I have made two revisions to the original Subjacency analysis given by Chomsky (1986a). First, I assume that aspectual auxiliaries such as *have* θ-mark (and therefore L-mark) VP. Second, I assume that a Spec-head agreement relation holds between the head and specifier of VP, which leads to the specifier of VP being L-marked by virtue of the L-marking of VP (this in contrast to the specifier of IP, which is in no way L-marked). This contrast supports the hypothesis that the two positions for the subject are in fact [Spec, IP] and [Spec, VP]. Thus, German subjects can appear in either the VP-external subject position ([Spec, IP]) or the VP-internal subject position ([Spec, VP]) at S-structure.[21]

In the next section I will return to these two sets of syntactic phenomena concerning the subject in German in considering once again the problem of deriving the logical representations from the S-structure representations. I will show that the German facts fill in a final piece of the argument justifying the Mapping Hypothesis.

2.4.2   Word Order and Subject Interpretations

So far, in justifying the tree-splitting algorithm for mapping S-structure representations into logical representations, I have shown that the two possible positions for the subject within the Kamp-Heim-style representations (in the nuclear scope and in a restrictive clause) do in fact correspond to two possible interpretations for subjects (the existential and generic readings of English bare plural subjects). I have also shown that the two syntactic positions for the subject ([Spec, IP] and [Spec, VP]) are clearly distinguished at S-structure in German, with sentential particles serving as a diagnostic for the position of the subject. Defining the position of the subject relative to the particles is further supported by extraction data (the *was-für* split and the split-topic construction). The task that remains is to show that the two syntactic positions illustrated by the German data directly correspond to the two positions in the logical representations illustrated by the English bare plural facts. To show this, I will now turn to the German bare plural.

German bare plural subjects, like the other German subjects we saw in the previous section, have the option of appearing in [Spec, VP] at S-structure rather than appearing in [Spec, IP], the two options being reflected in the relative word order. In the following examples (with stage-level predicates) the position of the subject is indicated relative to the position of the sentential particles.

(32) a. ... weil ja   doch Linguisten Kammermusik spielen.
            since PRT PRT   linguists   chamber music play
        '... since there are linguists playing chamber music.'

     b. ... weil Linguisten ja   doch Kammermusik spielen.
            since linguists   PRT PRT   chamber music play
        '... since (in general) linguists play chamber music.'

(33) a. ... weil ja   doch Haifische sichtbar sind.
            since PRT PRT   sharks   visible are
        '... since there are sharks visible.'

    b. ... weil Haifische ja   doch sichtbar sind.
        since sharks   PRT PRT   visible   are
      '... since (in general) sharks are visible.'

(34) a. ... weil ja   doch Kinder auf der Straße spielen.
        since PRT PRT   children on the street play
      '... since there are children playing in the street.'
    b. ... weil Kinder ja   doch auf der Straße spielen.
        since children PRT PRT   on the street play
      '... since (in general) children playing in the street.'

In the (a) examples the subject is in [Spec, VP], as shown by the fact that it is to the right of the particles *ja* and *doch*. In the (b) examples the subject is to the left of the particles, indicating that it is in [Spec, IP].

As the translations in the above examples show, the position of the bare plural subject makes a difference with respect to the relative availability of the generic and existential readings for the bare plural in German. The contrasting pairs of sentences in (32)–(34) show that the two possible positions for the bare plural subject (as indicated relative to the sentential particles) correspond to two different interpretations for the subject. The (a) examples have an existential reading (paraphrasable as a *there*-sentence), and the (b) sentences have a generic reading (paraphrasable with the sentential adverbial *in general*). Thus, in German the S-structure position of the subject correlates with the most readily available reading for a bare plural subject. A subject in [Spec, VP] yields the existential reading, and a subject in [Spec, IP] has the generic reading.

2.4.3 Word Order and the Stage/Individual Contrast

The correspondence between the S-structure position of the subject in German and its interpretation leads to a clear prediction concerning the subjects of stage- and individual-level predicates. Since stage-level predicates permit both the existential and generic readings, it is expected that the subject of a stage-level predicate should be able to appear in both [Spec, IP] and [Spec, VP] at S-structure in German. This is in fact what is seen in (32)–(34). (35)–(36) provide additional examples illustrating the contrast in interpretation that arises with stage-level predicates:

(35) a. ... weil Professoren ja doch verfügbar sind.
        since professors   'indeed' available are
      '... since (in general) professors are available.'

b. ... weil ja doch Professoren verfügbar sind.
     since 'indeed' professors   available are
'... since there are professors available.'

(36) a. ... weil Meerschweinchen ja doch mit der Bahn fahren
     since guinea pigs   'indeed' by train   travel
'... since (in general) guinea pigs travel by train.'

b. ... weil ja doch Meerschweinchen mit der Bahn fahren
     since 'indeed' guinea pigs   by train   travel
'... since there are guinea pigs traveling by train.'

With individual-level predicates, on the other hand, the bare plural subject can appear in the "outer" subject position to give a generic reading, but a bare plural subject to the right of the particles is somewhat awkward. (A more marked intonation pattern deaccenting the subject and stressing the predicate makes the awkward order more acceptable.) In any case, the existential reading is not possible, regardless of the intonation pattern:

(37) a.   ... weil Wildschweine ja doch intelligent sind.
     since wild boars   'indeed' intelligent are
'... since (in general) wild boars are intelligent.'

b. *?... weil ja doch Wildschweine intelligent sind.
     since 'indeed' wild boars   intelligent are

(38) a.   ... weil Skorpione ja doch giftig   sind.
     since scorpions 'indeed' poisonous are
'... since (in general) scorpions are poisonous.'

b. *?... weil ja doch Skorpione giftig   sind.
     since 'indeed' scorpions poisonous are

(39) a.   ... weil Wolfshunde   ja doch Deutsch können.
     since German shepherds 'indeed' German know
'... since (in general) German shepherds know German.'

b. *?... weil ja doch Wolfshunde   Deutsch können.
     since 'indeed' German shepherds German know

If, as I have claimed, the distinction between stage- and individual-level predicates is a syntactic distinction that restricts the position of the subject in individual-level predicates but not in stage-level predicates, then the facts in (37)–(39) are not unexpected. The (b) sentences are expected to be less good, since the subject of an individual-level predicate is base-generated in [Spec, IP], the outer position, and has no option of lowering into the VP. The impossibility of the generic reading follows from the Mapping Hypothesis. In order to receive an existential interpretation, a bare plural subject must be able to lower into the VP, where it will be mapped into the nuclear scope and bound by existential closure.

This then gives the final piece in the argument supporting the Mapping Hypothesis, or tree-splitting algorithm. The syntactic positions [Spec, IP] and [Spec, VP] correspond to the positions in the restrictive clause and the nuclear scope, respectively. This correspondence results in the contrast in interpretation observed in German sentences such as (32) and (33). Subjects in [Spec, VP] are mapped into the nuclear scope by tree splitting and are bound by existential closure to give the existential reading. The [Spec, IP] subjects, on the other hand, map into the restrictive clause and thereby receive the generic reading by virtue of being bound by the generic operator. The second result of this section is that unlike what happens in English, in German tree splitting can occur at S-structure. In other words, in deriving the logical representations for the sentences in (32) and (33), abstract movement operations such as LF lowering need not occur. This difference between German and English will be considered in more detail in chapter 3.

2.4.4 Extraction and the Stage/Individual Contrast

The two extraction constructions I introduced earlier give us another way of testing whether or not the syntactic formulation of the stage/individual contrast is correct. As I noted above, the *was-für* split and the split-topic construction are both sensitive to the position of a subject from which extraction occurs. If the subject is VP-internal, extraction is possible. If the subject is VP-external, extraction is not allowed.

Thus, it is predicted that extraction should be possible from the subjects of stage-level predicates, since these subjects have the option of appearing in the VP-internal subject position. Individual-level predicates, on the other hand, should disallow extraction from the subject, since they do not permit the option of having the subject in [Spec, VP].

This is in fact true for the *was-für* split. With individual-level predicates such as *intelligent* 'intelligent', *taub* 'deaf', *wasserdicht* 'waterproof', and *Französisch können* 'know French', the extraction is bad. With stage-level predicates such as *verfügbar* 'available' and *sichtbar* 'visible', and locative PPs such as *im Kühlschrank* 'in the refrigerator' and *auf der Straße* 'in the street', the extraction is permitted. This contrast is shown in (40)–(43).

(40) a. *Was sind für Leguane intelligent?
         what are for iguanas intelligent
         'What kind of iguanas are intelligent?'
     b. Was sind für Leguane verfügbar?
         what are for iguanas available
         'What kind of iguanas are available?'

(41) a. *Was sind für Abgottschlangen taub?
         what are for boa constrictors deaf
         'What kind of boa constrictors are deaf?'
     b. Was sind für Abgottschlangen sichtbar?
         what are for boa constrictors visible
         'What kind of boa constrictors are visible?'

(42) a. *Was sind für Schuhe wasserdicht?
         what are for shoes   waterproof
         'What kind of shoes are waterproof?'
     b. Was sind für Karotten im   Kühlschrank?
         what are for carrots   in-the refrigerator
         'What kind of carrots are in the refrigerator?'

(43) a. *Was können für Studenten Französisch?
         what know   for students   French
         'What kind of students know French?'
     b. Was sind für Tiere   auf der Straße?
         what are for animals on the street
         'What kind of animals are in the street?'

This type of extraction contrast between stage- and individual-level predicates also holds in the case of the split-topic construction. The stage-level predicates permit the fronting of the head noun of a subject NP, whereas the individual-level predicates do not:

(44) a. *Wildschweine sind viele intelligent.
         wild boars   are many intelligent
         'As for wild boars, many are intelligent.'
     b. Wildschweine sind viele verfügbar.
         wild boars   are many available
         'As for wild boars, many are available.'

(45) a. *Haifische sind viele taub.
         sharks   are many deaf
         'As for sharks, many are deaf.'

   b.   Haifische sind viele sichtbar.
         sharks   are many visible
         'As for sharks, many are visible.'

(46) a. *Schuhe sind viele wasserdicht.
         shoes   are many waterproof
         'As for shoes, many are waterproof.'

   b.   Karotten sind viele im   Kühlschrank.
         carrots   are many in-the refrigerator
         'As for carrots, many are in the refrigerator.'

(47) a. *Linguisten wissen das viele.
         linguists   know this many
         'As for linguists, many know this.'

   b.   Mücken   haben ihn viele gebissen.
         mosquitos have   him many bitten
         'As for mosquitos, many have bitten him.'

Thus, the extraction facts provide further support for the syntactic charac-
terization of the stage/individual contrast.

   In discussing the properties of stage- and individual-level predicates so far, I have purposely limited myself to the clearest cases of each type. Since the permanence of a property can vary with the particular context involved, the classification of a particular predicate may also vary. For instance, being red can be an individual-level property of strawberries, but when applied to a person it can be a stage-level property referring to a transitory state of blushing (this sort of variability in classification is similar to that seen in classifying a noun such as *wine* as a mass or count noun). In addition, there are many predicates that do not fall neatly into one category or the other. In the next section I will discuss a broader range of predicates and show that with a closer look, even in the more difficult cases the stage/individual classification is still useful in that it makes the important distinctions.

2.5   Delineating the Limits of the Predicate Classification

Although the most typical cases of stage- and individual-level predicates are fairly easy to classify by simply using the permanent- versus temporary-state distinction as a rule of thumb, there are numerous cases that cannot be classified as stage- or individual-level once and for all. The classification of predicates can vary, and not all predicates can be easily categorized in terms of permanent versus temporary states. Therefore, it is useful to consider some of the other properties that distinguish stage- and individual-level predicates in order to have a wider range of tests for distinguishing predicate types. Throughout the preceding discussion I have focused on two different properties of stage- and individual-level predicates. The first of these was semantic, concerning the interpretation of bare plural subjects. The second was syntactic, involving an extraction contrast. There are a number of other properties that distinguish the two predicate types. Another syntactic property is that *there*-insertion sentences are limited to stage-level predicates (Milsark 1974):

(48) a. There are carrots in the refrigerator.
     b. There are chili peppers available.
     c. There are pumpkins visible on the vine.

(49) a. *There are carrots nutritious.
     b. *There are chili peppers spicy.
     c. *There are pumpkins heavy.

In the following sections I will use these tests as well as others to examine some other predicate types that might be regarded as problematic for the approach I have taken. The problematic cases fall into a number of different semantic categories, which I will consider in turn.

2.5.1 Psychological States

Terms denoting psychological states of emotion such as *angry*, *cheerful*, *obnoxious*, *nervous*, and *nasty* might intuitively seem to be stage-level predicates in that they describe transitory states. However, applying the semantic and syntactic tests described above places them in the category of individual-level predicates. Consider the interpretation of the bare plural subjects in the following examples:

(50) a. Contrabassoonists are cheerful.
     b. Basenjis are nervous.
     c. Peasants are angry.
     d. Brussels sprouts are nasty.

In these sentences the bare plural subjects all have only the generic reading. This is typical of individual-level predicates.

   The psychological state predicates also behave somewhat like individual-level predicates with respect to the German extraction constructions:[22]

(51) a. *?Was sind für Trombonisten heiter?
          what are for trombonists   cheerful

   b. *?Was sind für Hunde nervös?
      what are for dogs   nervous
   c. *?Was sind für Kinder ungezogen?
      what are for children naughty

(52) a. *?Trombonisten sind viele heiter.
      trombonists   are many cheerful
   b. *?Hunde sind viele nervös.
      dogs   are many nervous
   c. *?Kinder sind viele ungezogen.
      children are many naughty

The extractions in the sentences in (51) and (52) are all rather awkward (if not downright ungrammatical), as would be expected if the subjects could only appear in the outer subject position from which extraction is prohibited.

   Finally, these predicates are also generally unacceptable in *there*-insertion contexts:

(53) a. *There are contrabassoonists cheerful.
   b. *There are Basenjis nervous.
   c. *There are Brussels sprouts nasty.

It looks, then, as if the intuitive rule of thumb regarding temporary states fails in these cases. There is a reason to take a closer look, however. I do not find the extractions in (51) and (52) as bad as the corresponding sentences with "canonical" individual-level predicates such as *intelligent*. There are contexts in which the extractions are quite acceptable. These are contexts where a temporal or spatial adverbial modifies the predicate. These interpretations are *not* possible for the more typical individual-level predicates:

(54) a. Kinder waren am Freitag viele nervös.
      children were   on Friday many nervous
      'As for children, many were nervous on Friday.'
   b. Trombonisten waren heute viele heiter.
      trombonists   were today many cheerful
      'As for trombonists, many were cheerful today.'

(55) a. *Kinder waren am Freitag viele intelligent.
      children were   on Friday many intelligent
   b. *Trombonisten waren heute viele blond.
      trombonists   were today many blond

Another fact about these predicates (noted by Stump (1985)) is that in English they become clearly stage-level (as indicated by the possibility of an existential interpretation for a bare plural subject) with a progressive form of *be*. This shifting of the predicate is less felicitous with the more typical individual-level predicates. The examples in (56) show the existential reading for the bare plural subjects.

(56) a. Contrabassoonists are being cheerful.
     b. Basenjis are being nervous.
     c. Peasants are being angry.

The observation that the stage-level interpretation is brought out in this context is supported by the fact that with the progressive *be* the states of emotion are also acceptable in *there*-insertion sentences:

(57) a. There are contrabassoonists being cheerful.
     b. There are Basenjis being nervous.
     c. There are peasants being angry.

What appears to be happening is that the psychological state predicates are in fact ambiguous in that certain contexts select an individual-level interpretation and others (in particular the progressive *be*) select a stage-level interpretation. This raises the question of just what the nature of this progressive *be* is. Carlson (1977b) notes that the progressive form of verbs usually goes hand in hand with the existential reading of a bare plural subject, whereas other verb forms are ambiguous between a habitual, or generic, interpretation and an existential interpretation:

(58) a. Basenjis yodel. (ambiguous)
     b. Basenjis are yodeling. (existential)

One possibility is that the progressive aspect is an indicator of the stage-level Infl, perhaps similar to the Spanish *be*-form *estar*, which selects stage-level predicates (as opposed to *ser*, which selects individual-level predicates).

A closer look shows that things are not as simple as that, however. The progressive *be* in the sentences in (56) is not permitted in all contexts. The most prominent restriction is that it requires an agentive subject:

(59) a. *Brussels sprouts are being nasty.
     b. *There are Brussels sprouts being nasty.

Thus, this form of the verb *be* is clearly Partee's (1977) "active" *be*. In other words, in the sentences in (56) the verb *be* takes a meaning roughly corresponding to 'act', and the adjectives have a more adverbial rather

than predicative function. This is true also when the progressive *be* com-
bines with more typical individual-level predicates such as *intelligent*:

(60) a.   Hector is being intelligent:
   b.   Horace is being stupid.
   c.   *?Hilda is being overweight.
   d.   *?Hepzibah is being tall.

Individual-level predicates that can modify *act* (such as *intelligent* and
stupid) are quite acceptable with the progressive *be*, as shown by (60a) and
(60b). Individual-level predicates that cannot readily modify *act* (such as
overweight and *tall*) are much less acceptable in this context.

In addition, the acceptable sentences in (60) allow *only* the adverbial
interpretation for the adjective. This adverbial interpretation is distinct
from the "transient property" interpretation found in stage-level predicates like *available*. In fact, truly stage-level predicates cannot readily
occur with the progressive *be*:

(61) a.   *Plumbers are being available.
   b.   *Saber-toothed tigers are being in the zoo.

This distinction between an adverbial interpretation and a truly stage-
level interpretation can be brought out by a "science fiction" example.[23]
One could devise imaginary contexts in which a predicate like *intelligent*
could have an interpretation that corresponds to a transient property. One
such context would be a planet where all beings are quite stupid, but they
have "intelligence pills" that enable them to be intelligent for a few hours
at a time, allowing them to complete their daily business. In this context
one could in fact say things like *Galrpthk is intelligent from 9 to 11*, much as
one can say *Bert is available from 9 to 11* here on Earth. The *there*-insertion
construction is also permitted in these cases: *There is a doctor intelligent in
this office at all times.*

This interpretation of *intelligent* is clearly distinct from the interpretation in (60a). Not only that, the science fiction context stage-level interpretations need not distinguish between predicates like *intelligent* and
overweight as the progressive *be* does.

These examples show not only that the behavior of these psychological
state predicates does in fact depend in part on tense and context, but also
that there is a distinction to be made between transitory properties that
are adverbial modifiers and the transient quality found in the most typical
stage-level predicates. Thus, in some contexts the states-of-emotion predicates are strongly individual-level and in others they function as adverbial

modifiers to the progressive *be*, taking on certain stage-level properties. This variability is what results in the somewhat counterintuitive judgments in (50)–(53). The states of emotion are capable of being both permanent characteristics (as in (50)–(53)) and transitory modifiers (as when applied to the English progressive form, or when appearing with an overt adverbial in German).

2.5.2 Individual-Level Unaccusatives

As I noted earlier, Kratzer (1989) observes that there is a class of individual-level predicates whose subjects are generated in an *internal* (object) position. Unlike stage-level predicates, which can also have internal subjects, these predicates do not give evidence of having the abstract spatiotemporal event argument. Expressed in terms of the analysis I have given, these predicates are those that do not have the event argument and also do not assign a θ-role to [Spec, IP] (see the chart in (20)). Examples of predicates of this type are *be known to*, *belongs to*, *be similar to*, and *be familiar to*. This classification corresponds roughly to the "possessional locative" predicates of Gruber (1965) and Jackendoff (1972).

In order to see more clearly how these predicates are distinguished from the canonical stage- and individual-level predicates, it is useful to consider Kratzer's diagnostics for the presence of an event argument. One of her arguments involves locative modifiers. She observes that these modifiers can only modify stage-level predicates. With regard to this test the individual-level unaccusatives pattern with individual-level predicates in that they do not permit a locative to modify the predicate. It can only modify the noun, as shown by the translations in (62). The translation corresponding to predicate modification is not possible.

(62) a.   ... weil alle Skorpione in dieser Wüste giftig   sind.
                   since all scorpions in this   desert poisonous are
         '... since all scorpions in this desert are poisonous.'
       *'... since all scorpions are poisonous in this desert.'
     b.   ... weil mir   alle Skorpione in dieser Wüste gehören.
                   since to-me all scorpions in this   desert belong
         '... since all scorpions in this desert belong to me.'
       *'... since all scorpions belong to me in this desert.'

This contrasts with the clearly stage-level predicates that permit the locative to modify either the noun or the predicate itself:

(63) ... weil ihn alle Skorpione in dieser Wüste gebissen haben.
      since him all scorpions in this desert bitten have
   '... since all the scorpions in this desert have bitten him.'
   '... since all the scorpions have bitten him in this desert.'

Kratzer claims that the predicate modification in (63) results from the locative expression relating to the verb via the event argument. In the absence of this argument, as in the sentences in (62), this modification is not possible. Thus, example (62b) shows that predicates like *belong to* do not have the event argument, and that they pattern with individual-level predicates like *is poisonous*.

    The claim that these predicates are "unaccusative" in the sense that their subjects are generated VP-internally is supported by the extraction facts. Unlike typical individual-level predicates, the individual-level unaccusatives permit extraction from their subjects:

(64) a. Skorpione gehören ihm viele.
      scorpions belong to-him many
      'As for scorpions, many belong to him.'
   b. Giftige Skorpione sind mir viele bekannt.
      poisonous scorpions are to-me many known
      'As for poisonous scorpions, many are known to me.'

The individual-level unaccusatives also are permitted in *there*-insertion constructions:

(65) a. There are counterexamples known to me.
   b. There are some scorpions belonging to Simon.
   c. There are presidents similar to Millard Fillmore.
   d. There are many marsupials familiar to Marvin.

    Thus, although predicates such as *be known to* and *belong to* denote permanent or individual-level properties, they also show some of the syntactic and semantic properties of stage-level predicates. This apparent mismatch is resolved if the properties that distinguish stage- and individual-level predicates (the event argument and θ-role assignment to [Spec, IP] in my account) are allowed to vary independently.

2.5.3 Experiencers

Another class of verbs that requires special mention is the *experiencer* type. These are individual-level predicates (describing more or less permanent properties) that also induce generic readings of bare plural *objects*. Examples of verbs of this type are *appreciate, loathe, love,* and *like:*

(66) a. Professors appreciate neatly written papers.

    b. Children loathe Brussels sprouts.

    c. Scottish Highland cattle love windy days.

    d. Chinchillas like dried currants.

Taking the Mapping Hypothesis quite literally, the generic readings of the objects in (66) are unexpected, since the VP (and the bare plural contained within it) should be mapped into the nuclear scope, and the bare plural should be bound by existential closure to give an existential reading for the object. Instead, both the subject and the object seem to be mapped into a restrictive clause where both are bound by the generic operator:

(67) a. $\text{Gen}_{x,y}$ [x is a professor $\wedge$ y is a neat paper] x appreciates y

    b. $\text{Gen}_{x,y}$ [x is a child $\wedge$ y is a Brussels sprout] x hates y

    c. $\text{Gen}_{x,y}$ [x is a Scottish Highland cow $\wedge$ y is a windy day] x loves y

As I mentioned earlier, what seems to be happening is that the bare plural objects scramble at LF to adjoin to IP, and then are mapped into a restrictive clause by the tree-splitting algorithm. I will not discuss this phenomenon any further here, since I deal with both LF scrambling of objects and the semantic properties of experiencer verbs in chapters 3 and 4.

2.5.4 Contextual Effects

Finally, the stage/individual distinction is obviously subject to contextual influences, even in cases other than the psychological states discussed above. Predicates that are of one category in a somewhat neutral context can be pushed into the other category in various ways. A group of problematic cases of this type includes predicates like *sick* and *drunk*. These are generally thought of as stage-level predicates (see Milsark 1974 and Carlson 1977b):

(68) a. There are children sick.

    b. There are people drunk.

(69) a. Children are sick.

    b. People are drunk.

In (68) and (69) the predicates *sick* and *drunk* behave like stage-level predicates—they are permitted in the *there*-insertion sentences, and they allow both existential and generic readings for bare plural subjects.

Adding descriptive material to the subject NPs changes the behavior of these predicates, however. In this case the predicates can behave like individual-level predicates in that they are prohibited in *there*-insertion contexts and strongly favor the generic reading of the subject, in contrast to a "canonical" stage-level predicate such as *available*:

(70) a. *There are children with red rashes sick.
     b. *There are people in bars drunk.
     c.   There are children with red rashes available.
     d.   There are people in bars available.

(71) a.   Children with red rashes are sick.
     b.   People in bars are drunk.
     c.   Children with red rashes are available.
     d.   People in bars are available.

Thus, with certain stage-level predicates like *sick* and *drunk* additional descriptive content in the subject NP can force restrictive clause formation and subsequent binding by the generic operator. In chapter 3 I will discuss this property of more "specific" NPs and show that restrictive clause formation of this type is a quite general process, extending to all indefinites.

2.6   Focus and the Bare Plural Readings

At various points in this chapter I have mentioned that intonational factors can play a role in the matter of the interpretation of bare plurals, and in the case of German, intonation can also be regarded as a factor influencing word order. In this section I will give speculative consideration to the role that focus and intonation play in "semantic partition," and to how certain focus phenomena can be accounted for within the framework developed here. I make no attempt to develop a comprehensive theory of focus phenomena, since that would take me beyond the scope of this monograph, but I present some remarks that might suggest a direction in which future research could proceed.

   Setting aside the question of German word order for the time being, I consider first the role of focus in the interpretation of bare plural subjects. Recall that stage-level predicates allow three readings for a bare plural subject:

(72) a. Firemen are available.
     b. $\exists_x$ x is a fireman $\wedge$ x is available
     c. $\text{Gen}_{x,t}$ [x is a fireman $\wedge$ t is a time] x is available at t
     d. Gen_t [t is a time] $\exists_x$ x is a fireman $\wedge$ x is available at t

Although all three of these readings are generally possible, focusing various constituents can cause certain readings to be favored over the others.

The judgments in many cases are subtle, but I find for example that focusing the subject leads to favoring the existential reading represented in (72b), and that focusing the adjective leads to favoring the generic reading represented in (72c):

(73) a. FIREMEN are available.
     b. Firemen are AVAILABLE.

At first blush, this phenomenon may appear to present a counterexample to the central claim that I am arguing for in this work—namely, that syntactic structure is a major determinant of the semantic partition of a sentence—in that the focus structure appears to be delineating the two parts of the logical representation. For example, on a focus-oriented account the sentences in (73) could perhaps be (roughly) mapped into their logical representations by mapping the focus material into the nuclear scope, and extrafocal material into the restrictive clause, rather than making a syntactic division of the sentence.

But simply noting the correspondence between focus structure and the structure of the logical representation in the sentences in (73) is not sufficient to dismiss the Mapping Hypothesis. What is most important to bear in mind at this point is that focus is not the *only* determinant of the readings. The patterns of focus shown in (73) are not in fact necessary to induce the readings they favor. In appropriate contexts, any one of the possible readings can also arise with neutral focus. Thus, although focus certainly can have an effect on the interpretation of a particular utterance, it is not an essential component of any particular interpretation. Consequently, focusing contrasts such as that illustrated by the examples (73a) and (73b) do not in and of themselves constitute counterexamples to the proposal that the syntactic structure of the sentence plays an important role in determining its semantic partition.

A second reason not to dismiss the Mapping Hypothesis in favor of a focus-based account is that it is not clear that focus phenomena cannot also be accounted for within the syntactic account. In fact, certain focus phenomena concerning stage- and individual-level predicates appear to provide additional support for the syntax-oriented approach I have taken here.

The observation brought out by the interpretive preferences in (73) is roughly that the "focus part" of the sentence corresponds to the nuclear scope of the logical representation, and the extrafocal portion corresponds to the restrictive clause. This observation can be recast in terms of the tree-splitting approach by saying that in sentences like (73a) focus on the subject causes the subject to lower into the [Spec, VP] position at LF; consequently, when tree splitting applies, the subject is mapped into the nuclear scope, yielding the existential reading. Thus, the effect of focus in this case is that it causes the subject to move into the VP domain at LF. Support for this characterization of the effect of focus comes from certain data concerning the operation of "focus projection."

Focus projection is the process by which focus (which is assumed to be some kind of feature that appears on a word or phrase; see, for example, Chomsky 1971, Jackendoff 1972, and Selkirk 1984) is projected (or percolated) upward from the word that receives the pitch accent. The fact that focus can project upward to produce "focus domains" of varying size is most clearly brought out in association with operators like *only* and *even* (Jackendoff 1972, Rooth 1985):

(74) a. I only ate [CABBAGE].
     b. I only [ate CABBAGE].

In the sentence in (74) I have indicated the domain of the projected focus by square brackets. Thus, focus can project either to the NP (74a) or up to the VP (74b). Projecting focus to the NP gives a "contrastive" reading that can be paraphrased as 'The only thing I ate was cabbage'. The reading in (74b) can be paraphrased as 'The only thing I did today was eat cabbage'.

Focus projection is subject to a number of constraints, the one most relevant here being that in most cases focus projection beyond a subject NP is not possible:

(75) a. I only said that [BERT] likes Brussels sprouts.
     b. *I only said that [BERT likes Brussels sprouts].

With focus on *Bert* in the sentence in (75), only the contrastive reading in (75a), paraphrased as 'I only said that Bert likes Brussels sprouts, not that Betty (or anyone else) does', is possible. The reading with focus projected over the entire embedded sentence, as in (75b), is not possible. The sentence cannot mean 'The only thing I said was that Bert likes Brussels sprouts, I didn't say anything else'.

Selkirk (1984) notes that there are exceptions to the prohibition on projecting focus beyond subjects. Most notably, subjects of unaccusatives allow focus projection beyond the subject NP:

(76) a. The chicken only said that [the SKY] is falling.
     b. The chicken only said that [the SKY is falling].

Thus, it appears that when the subject is base-generated from a VP-internal position, then focus projection from a subject NP over an entire clause is allowed. Therefore, it is not surprising that stage- and individual-level predicates contrast with respect to focus projection (see also Gussenhoven 1984):

(77) a.   Betty only said that [EGGPLANTS are available].
     b. *Betty only said that [EGGPLANTS are poisonous].

Stage-level predicates allow focus projection from a subject NP, whereas individual-level predicates do not.

The generalization concerning focus projection seems to be that focus can project from a phrase that has been base-generated within VP, but not from a phrase generated outside of VP. If there is a correspondence between the nuclear scope and the projected focus domain, as I suggested above, it is not surprising that only subjects that can lower into [Spec, VP] permit projection of focus over the whole sentence. Put in another way, the effect of focus on the subjects in (76a) and (77a) (as well as (73a)) is that it forces the subjects to "lower" into the VP (presumably at LF). Thus, the correspondence between the VP and the nuclear scope can still be maintained, a result that is given additional support by the focus projection data.

This hypothesis concerning the effects of focusing may also account for the observations I made above concerning focus and word order in German. Recall that there is a contrast between stage- and individual-level predicates with respect to possible word orders:

(78) a.   ... weil Professoren ja doch verfügbar sind.
             since professors 'indeed' available are
          '... since (in general) professors are available.'
     b.   ... weil ja doch Professoren verfügbar sind.
             since 'indeed' professors   available are
          '... since there are professors available.'

(79) a.   ... weil Skorpione ja doch giftig   sind.
             since scorpions 'indeed' poisonous are
          '... since (in general) scorpions are poisonous.'
     b. *?... weil ja doch Skorpione giftig   sind.
             since 'indeed' scorpions poisonous are

I also remarked above that deaccenting the subject and stressing the predicate makes the word order in (79b) more acceptable, although the subject can only receive a generic interpretation (see also Lenerz 1977,

Lötscher 1983, and Jacobs 1984 for further discussion of focus and word order in German):

(80) ... weil ja doch Skorpione GIFTIG sind.
　　　 since 'indeed' scorpions poisonous are
　　 '... since (in general) scorpions are poisonous.'

Since the subject of *poisonous* is base-generated in [Spec, IP], it is not surprising that it cannot be focused, since then it would be forced to lower into [Spec, VP]. The puzzling fact is that the subject appears to be VP-internal in (80), based on its position relative to the particles. This might perhaps be explained by the fact that German allows scrambling, which reorders constituents (including adverbials) by adjoining them to IP (Webelhuth 1989; see also the discussion and references cited in chapters 3 and 4). Thus, the order in (80) may arise not from the subject being VP-internal, but from scrambling of the particles *ja* and *doch*, a conjecture that would be consistent with both the intonation pattern required and the generic interpretation that results.

These remarks are not conclusive by any means, and of course certain questions still remain. An obvious question concerns the correspondence between the nuclear scope and the focus: why should this correspondence exist? Another is how to handle sentences in which the focused part does not include the whole VP.[24] Both of these questions relate to the issue of the role the restrictive clause plays in representing presupposed (in this context, nonfocal) material within the sentence. In chapter 3 I explore the significance of presuppositionality with regard to restrictive clause formation. In particular, I introduce a syntactic mechanism of *presupposition accommodation* (following work by Berman (1991); and see also Partee, to appear, for an application to focus phenomena). This mechanism (which basically incorporates presupposed, or nonfocused, material into a restrictive clause via a syntactic rule of quantifier raising) may provide a basis by which the relationship of focus to the interpretation of indefinite NPs can be accounted for by the (syntactic) Mapping Hypothesis.

2.7　Conclusion

In this chapter I demonstrated that there is support in both English and German for the Mapping Hypothesis. The interpretations of the English bare plural provide evidence for the two positions for the subject in the logical representation, and the German data provide evidence for the correspondence between the two positions in the logical representation and the two readings of the bare plural subject. The existence of two S-structure subject positions in German is supported by the *was-für* and split-topic extraction facts.

The contrasts between stage- and individual-level predicates in both languages also support the correspondence between the two syntactic subject positions and the two positions in the logical representations. Here the possibility of the existential, or "internal," reading correlates with the possibility of extraction. I have suggested that the two predicate types are distinguished by two parameters, θ-role assignment to [Spec, IP] and the presence/absence of a "Davidsonian" event argument (following Kratzer (1989)).

Finally, I discussed a number of cases that seem to present problems for a simple two-way division of predicate types. I showed that these difficulties can be accommodated by a number of different means. Although some predicate types require additional variation in the two parameters differentiating predicate types (e.g., the individual-level unaccusatives), other predicates (those involving states of emotion) seem to have two distinct stage-level and individual-level forms. Finally, for a number of stage-level predicates context plays an important role in determining which interpretation of a bare plural subject (the generic or the existential) is preferred.

In this chapter I have limited myself to discussing the interpretation of bare plural subjects. In chapter 3 I extend the Mapping Hypothesis to NPs of other types. I show that many of these also admit of two interpretations, one corresponding to a tripartite quantificational structure and the other corresponding to binding by existential closure. I also discuss the interpretation of object NPs and consider the relationship between restrictive clause structures and the operation of the rule of QR proposed by May (1977, 1985).

Chapter 3
Tree Splitting and the
Interpretation of Indefinites

3.1 Introduction

In the previous chapter I introduced the Mapping Hypothesis and showed how it explained a number of facts concerning the interpretation of a particular type of NP—the bare plural—in English and German. In this chapter I extend my analysis to indefinite and quantificational NPs in general. Taking Kamp's (1981) and Heim's (1982) analyses of the interpretation of indefinites as my starting point, I propose that there are actually two types of indefinites (rather than treating them uniformly, as Kamp and Heim do): those that form restrictive clause structures, and those that are bound by existential closure. The syntactic nature of the derivation of the tripartite logical representations (as represented by the tree-splitting algorithm) leads to the consequence that these two types of indefinites are themselves distinguished syntactically by the operation of the rule of QR (May 1977, 1985).

3.2 Tree Splitting and Quantification

The tree-splitting algorithm has a number of syntactic and semantic consequences for a theory of quantification. As a result of the formation of the restrictive clause and nuclear scope by dividing the tree into two parts, the categories IP and VP are distinguished in the derivation of logical representations as domains for different kinds of quantification, and thus IP subjects and VP subjects are also semantically differentiated. In the rest of this chapter I take a closer look at quantification and the Kamp-Heim theory of indefinites in light of the Mapping Hypothesis that I have proposed. I show that indefinites are actually ambiguous between presuppositional and nonpresuppositional readings (as originally observed by

Milsark (1974)). Rather than presenting a problem for a theory that represents indefinites as variables (an objection in fact raised by De Hoop and De Swart (1990)), this ambiguity can be neatly represented in a Kamp-Heim framework by the IP/VP contrast coupled with the tree-splitting procedure.

3.2.1 Some Consequences of Tree Splitting

The first step in examining quantification in the context of the tree-splitting procedure for mapping to logical representations is to step back and take a look at where and how this proposal deviates from the original Kamp-Heim theory of the interpretation of indefinites. The first point of departure involves the domain of existential closure. I claimed that the domain of existential closure should be defined in sentential terms as the VP of the sentence. In other words, only nuclear scopes (which correspond to VPs, by the Mapping Hypothesis) are subject to existential closure. This contrasts with the original Kamp-Heim theory, in which existential closure applies to sentences, and an additional existential closure operation applies to the entire text, or discourse.

Restricting existential closure to nuclear scopes was initially motivated in chapter 2 by the interpretation of bare plurals generated outside VP (as in the case of subjects of individual-level predicates). These NPs can never receive an existential interpretation, and this observation led to the claim that they must be outside the domain of existential closure. Permitting existential closure of texts as well as nuclear scopes would make it impossible to maintain this result.

Independent arguments against the original Kamp-Heim approach to existential closure have also been given by Kadmon (1987), Heim (1990), and Kratzer (1989).[1] I will take Kadmon's observations as my starting point in this discussion. Kadmon uses examples from Evans 1977 to argue that existential closure of texts makes incorrect predictions regarding the binding of pronouns that are not c-commanded by their antecedents, such as in (1).

(1) Oscar owns sheep. Otto vaccinates them.

Existential closure applied to the text in (1) yields the interpretation that Oscar owns sheep that Otto vaccinates, as shown in the representation in (2).

(2) $\exists_x$ [x is a sheep $\wedge$ Oscar owns x $\wedge$ Otto vaccinates x]

The reason that (2) does not correctly represent the meaning of the text in

(1) is that on its most natural reading (1) carries the implication that Otto vaccinates *all* of Oscar's sheep, or that Otto vaccinates whatever sheep Oscar owns. (Kadmon calls this implication the "Uniqueness/Maximality Effect.") The logical representation in (2) (in which the pronoun is bound by existential closure applying to the whole text) merely asserts that there are *some* sheep owned by Oscar and vaccinated by Otto. This interpretation does not necessarily yield the implication carried by the actual text in (1)—the logical representation in (2) could be true if there are some sheep that Oscar owns that Otto doesn't vaccinate. The argument against existential closure of texts rests on the observation that if pronouns such as *them* in (1) are analyzed in some way other than being bound by a discourse-level operation of existential closure, this problem in the logical representation does not arise. The question then is how to represent these pronouns.

One possibility is that developed by Kadmon. She argues that all definites that are not syntactically (i.e., c-command) bound must refer to some unique set or another. The variation on this approach that I will take here is to limit existential closure to nuclear scopes only and to simply give pronouns such as *them* in example (1) the analysis proposed by Evans (1977) for these cases. Evans calls these pronouns "E-type" pronouns. As illustrated above, these are pronouns that are anaphorically related to NPs that do not c-command them. (For example, in (1) *them* is related to *sheep* in the preceding sentence.) Evans treats E-type pronouns as definite descriptions, so that *them* in (1) corresponds to 'the sheep that Oscar owns'. With this type of analysis, we no longer need existential closure of texts, since the correct anaphoric relations between pronouns and their non-c-commanding antecedents will be given by the E-type analysis.[2] Therefore, I will simply take examples such as (1) as additional evidence that there is *no* existential closure of texts, and that existential closure applies to nuclear scopes (or VPs) only, as implied by the tree-splitting algorithm.

This restricting of the operation of existential closure to nuclear scopes leads to a second important consequence of the Mapping Hypothesis concerning a constraint on the interpretation of indefinites. If the nuclear scope of the logical representation is formed from the VP of a sentence, as claimed in the Mapping Hypothesis, then a clear prediction is made regarding the syntactic distribution of indefinites that lack quantificational force. All existential, nongeneric indefinite NPs that have no quantificational force of their own must be within the VP after tree splitting applies (whether at LF or S-structure).[3] This is so that they can receive existential force from existential closure, which applies only to nuclear scopes, or VPs. (The indefinite determiners in these cases function as cardinality predicates applied to the variable introduced by the NP.) If they were to remain external to the VP, the variables introduced by these NPs would remain unbound.

The correctness of this consequence of the Mapping Hypothesis clearly depends on which NPs are said to have no quantificational force. In the original Kamp-Heim theory *all* indefinites are claimed to be without quantificational force. If this were actually the case, the following sentence would be ungrammatical:

(3) ... weil zwei Kinder ja doch auf der Straße spielen.
    since two children 'indeed' in the street play

The sentence in (3) should be bad because the subject NP *zwei Kinder* 'two children' is a nongeneric indefinite (and therefore without quantificational force, according to Heim (1982)), and it is *external* to the VP, as indicated by the fact that it appears to the left of the particles *ja* and *doch*. Since the mapping to logical representations (tree splitting) in German in cases like (3) does not involve any LF lowering of the subject NP (recall the discussion in chapter 2), the subject NP will not end up in the domain of existential closure, since it will not be mapped into a nuclear scope because it is not contained in the VP. However, contrary to prediction, the sentence in (3) is perfectly grammatical. If the Mapping Hypothesis is correct, the indefinite NP in (3) must in fact have quantificational force of its own. In other words, the indefinite must be able to form a restrictive clause, with the determiner *zwei* 'two' functioning as an operator binding the variable introduced in the restrictive clause, rather than functioning as a cardinality predicate.

Thus, the original Kamp-Heim conception of indefinites as being uniformly without quantificational force is not compatible with the Mapping Hypothesis that I have proposed. In order to maintain the Mapping Hypothesis, we need to reconsider the classification of indefinites. Specifically, we need (at least) *two* types of indefinites. In addition to indefinites with no quantificational force of their own (cardinality predicates, or traditional Kamp-Heim indefinites), which receive existential force from existential closure, we need indefinites that have quantificational force and form operator-variable structures by introducing a restrictive clause. In the next section I present an alternative to the original Kamp-Heim view of indefinites (based on the work of Milsark (1974)) that meets these requirements. This classification not only allows us to maintain the Mapping Hypothesis, but also provides additional support for it.

3.2.2 Ambiguous Indefinites and Milsark's Classification

The idea that indefinites might have multiple interpretations is certainly not a novel one. Milsark (1974) distinguishes two types of determiners, which he calls *strong* and *weak*, and gives a syntactic diagnostic for distinguishing between them. Weak determiners can appear with a subject NP in *there*-insertion contexts, whereas strong determiners cannot (the so-called definiteness effect). This is shown in the examples in (4).

(4) a.   There is/are a/some/a few/many/three fly (flies) in my soup.
    b.   *There is/are the/every/all/most fly (flies) in my soup.

These examples show that the determiners *a*, *some*, *a few*, and *many* are all weak determiners. Also included in this class are the numerals, such as *three*. The strong determiners include *the*, *every*, *all*, and *most*, as shown by the fact that they are ungrammatical in the *there*-insertion context given in (4b).

Milsark also describes what he calls a semantic distinction between the two types of determiners. This distinction centers on the notion of presuppositionality. Strong determiners presuppose the existence of the entities they are applied to. Weak determiners are ambiguous between a presuppositional reading and a nonpresuppositional reading in which they merely assert the existence of whatever entities they are applied to.[4] This ambiguity of weak quantifiers can be seen in (5).[5]

(5) a.   There are some ghosts in my house. (unstressed *some*, asserts existence of ghosts)
    b.   SOME ghosts are in the pantry; the others are in the attic. (presupposes the existence of ghosts)

In (5a) the nonpresuppositional, or cardinal, reading of the determiner *some* is shown. In this sentence the determiner *some* is unstressed, and the sentence simply asserts the existence of ghosts in my house (in *there*-insertion contexts such as (5a) the cardinal reading of a weak determiner is in fact the only reading possible). If there are ghosts, the sentence is true. If ghosts turn out not to exist, the sentence will be false. In (5b) the determiner is stressed, and the presuppositional reading is most salient. This sentence presupposes the existence of ghosts. If no ghosts exist, the sentence will not be straightforwardly false; its truth-value will be undefined. The presuppositional reading, unlike the cardinal reading, can be paraphrased as a partitive: 'three of the ghosts'.[6]

Strong determiners, on the other hand, are unambiguous. They permit only the presuppositional reading. The cardinal reading is not possible, as shown by the sentences in (6).

(6) a. Every ghost roasted marshmallows.

  b. Most ghosts sleep late.

Both the sentences in (6) carry the presupposition that ghosts must in fact exist. In the absence of ghosts the sentences have no truth-value.

In summary, Milsark proposes to group determiners into two classes. The first class, the strong determiners, consists of those determiners that are unambiguously presuppositional and produce ungrammaticality in *there*-insertion contexts. The second group, the weak determiners, are ambiguous between a cardinal and a presuppositional reading. And unlike the strong determiners, the weak determiners are acceptable in *there*-insertion sentences. In this context only the cardinal reading is possible.

The question that remains is, How does this classification of determiners get us out of the dilemma concerning indefinites that I noted in the previous section? Recall that the problem was that the tree-splitting procedure for deriving logical representations forced us into a position where we needed two types of indefinites, those with quantificational force of their own, and those without quantificational force. This conclusion was forced by the fact that not all indefinites need to be within the VP at the point of tree splitting, as shown by the German data. In the next section I attempt to resolve this dilemma by means of investigating the connection between Milsark's semantic classification of determiners and the syntactic properties of the tree-splitting algorithm.

3.2.3 Presuppositions and the Syntax of Determiners

The proposed syntactic basis for the components of the logical representation points toward a syntactic account of Milsark's semantic distinction between strong and weak determiners. The hypothesis that I wish to investigate here is that strong and weak determiners differ with respect to how they are treated at the level of LF (or the level at which tree splitting occurs). This involves amalgamating recent ideas concerning the role of presuppositions in semantic representations (following Heim (1983) and Berman (1991)) with commonly held assumptions about the syntax of quantifier scope.

In the Government-Binding Theory scope relations are represented through the use of movement rules that apply at the level of LF. Specifically, May (1977, 1985) has proposed that the scope domains of quantified NPs are represented by means of the movement rule QR, which adjoins the quantified NPs to IP. The scope domain of the quantifier consists of the nodes it c-commands from its raised position, and the raised NP leaves behind a trace that it binds from its raised position.[7] One interesting property of May's account, and of most other analyses assuming a movement-based approach to quantifier scope representation, is that all quantifiers (both strong and weak) are treated equally by QR.[8]

I would like to suggest here that the strong and weak determiners actually differ with respect to QR. Strongly quantified NPs behave like quantified NPs in May's account. They are raised by QR to adjoin to IP. When tree splitting applies, they form a tripartite quantificational structure consisting of an operator (the quantifier), a restrictive clause, and a nuclear scope. Weak quantifiers, on the other hand, are ambiguous. On their cardinal reading, they do not induce QR (in the sense of adjoining to IP). NPs with weak quantifiers may remain within the VP, functioning as cardinality predicates that introduce variables that are given existential force by existential closure. Thus, a cardinality predicate, in conjunction with existential closure, asserts the existence of a set whose size is specified by the determiner (the "size" of sets introduced by relative determiners such as *few* and *many* will of course be contextually determined).[9] On their presuppositional reading the weak quantifiers behave just like strong quantifiers. They are raised to IP by QR, and they form a tripartite quantificational structure.[10]

At this point two immediate consequences of this proposal become evident. The first is that the syntactic distribution of indefinites is explained. There is no longer any mystery about why the following sentence is grammatical:

(7) ... weil zwei Kinder ja doch auf der Straße spielen.
　　　　 since two children 'indeed' in the street play

In the analysis presented here the indefinite NP *zwei Kinder* 'two children' can have two readings, since the numeral *zwei* 'two' is a weak determiner. On its cardinal reading it would have no quantificational force and would therefore have to remain in the VP. But it can also have a presuppositional reading, due to the ambiguity of weak determiners. On this reading it maps into a restrictive clause, and therefore not only *can* be external to the VP, but at some level *must* be external to the VP. The presuppositional reading is in fact the only reading possible in (7). (I will discuss the distribution of the various readings of indefinites in German in more detail below.)

A second consequence is that the relationship between the presuppositional nature of the "strong" readings and restrictive clause formation is given a syntactic characterization. To see how this works, we need to consider first the role of the restrictive clause in the logical representation and how it relates to the notion of presupposition that I have been using to characterize what we might now call the *quantifier-raising (QR) reading* of indefinites.

Generally, in a tripartite logical representation the restrictive clause defines a set that the quantifier quantifies over.[11] If this set is empty, the truth-conditions for the sentence will be undefined. Thus, the set defined by the restrictive clause can be taken to represent the existence presupposition induced by the quantifier. In other words, the presuppositions induced by the quantifier are somehow incorporated into the restrictive clause.

The hypothesis that the presuppositions of a quantified sentence are represented in the restrictive clause is also discussed by Berman (1991), who assimilates the process of restrictive clause formation to the notion of presupposition accommodation of Lewis (1979).[12] The basic idea behind presupposition accommodation is that conversations involve a "conversational background" of information that the conversational participants take for granted. Accommodation is the process by which this background is "updated"—additional information is incorporated into the conversational background as new presuppositions become apparent. To give a concrete example, if I say to a friend who up to that point has been unaware of the specifics of my eating habits "I am going to give up eating Brussels sprouts," my friend will automatically accommodate the presupposition that I did until that time eat Brussels sprouts and will thereby be able to interpret my sentence. (This is admittedly a rather informal description; for a more formal account, see Heim 1983.) The claim made by Berman (in the context of the semantics of questions) is that the incorporation of presuppositions of a quantified sentence into the restrictive clause is simply another instance of this sort of presupposition accommodation.

The Mapping Hypothesis, along with the tree-splitting procedure that forms the restrictive clause from IP-level material, leads to the conclusion that in the case of quantified NPs this process of accommodation is essentially syntactic in nature, mediated by the rule of QR. Following Berman, then, the presuppositions induced by quantified NPs must be incorporated into a restrictive clause. Thus, presuppositional NPs that are within VP at S-structure must be raised to IP by QR at the level at which tree splitting takes place in order to be mapped into a restrictive clause. (Note that tree splitting in English clearly always takes place at LF. I will discuss the case of other languages such as German in chapter 4.)

A concrete example of how this works can be seen in the case of a "strong" interpretation of a quantified object NP. The presupposition of existence induced by the "strong" reading is reflected in the formation of a restrictive clause. This restrictive clause formation can in turn be regarded as a syntactic property, since the formation of a restrictive clause is the result of having raised the NP (by QR) to adjoin to IP, as required by the Mapping Hypothesis. A further consequence of the tree-splitting algorithm is that NPs that are not raised to the IP level do not induce the formation of a restrictive clause. Thus, Milsark's presuppositional/cardinal distinction has a syntactic representation (with respect to whether or not QR applies) at the level at which tree splitting occurs.

3.2.4   The Strong/Weak Distinction and Relative Scope
Deriving Milsark's strong/weak distinction from the presence or absence of restrictive clause formation through QR also has a number of consequences with regard to relative scope determination. The first consequence concerns the actual relative scope predictions for particular determiners in multiply-quantified sentences. Whereas most syntactic accounts of quantifier scope phenomena treat quantifiers equally with respect to relative scope, the account I have outlined makes a clear differential prediction with regard to different quantifier types (see also Kroch 1974 and Ioup 1975 for accounts of relative quantifier scope based on scope order preferences rather than syntactic movement operations). In a sentence with a *weakly* quantified subject (on its cardinal reading) and a *strongly* quantified object (presuppositional), the object should receive wider scope than the subject.

(8) a. Sm cellists played every suite today.
    b. Mny cellists played SOME suite today.
    c. Tw cellists played SOME suite today.

In the sentences in (8) the strongly quantified object NPs *every suite* and *some suite* take scope over the weakly quantified subject NPs. (I indicate the unstressed readings of the determiners by deleting the vowels.) The syntactic account of the strong/weak distinction derives this relative scoping in a fairly straightforward way. The presuppositional object NPs are raised to IP at LF by QR, where they form a restrictive clause by tree splitting. In contrast, the cardinal subject NP lowers at LF back into [Spec, VP], where it can receive existential force by existential closure. Thus, the object NP takes wider (IP) scope than the subject NP, which is confined to VP.[13]

This variation in scope preference conforms with other observations in the literature on relative scope. In a discussion of the factors that determine relative quantifier scope, Ioup (1975) notes that the various quantifiers differ in relative scope preferences. Ioup represents these varying relative scope preferences among quantifiers in the form of a hierarchy. The leftmost elements in the hierarchy show the greatest preference for wider scope, and the rightmost elements show the greatest preference for narrower scope:

(9) *Ioup's hierarchy*
   each > every > all > most > many > several > some > a few

This hierarchy bears an interesting relationship to Milsark's classification. If the hierarchy in (9) is bisected, the quantifiers in the left-hand half (those tending toward wider scope) all fall into the class of strong determiners, and those in the right-hand half (those tending toward narrower scope) all fall into the class of weak quantifiers. Thus, in a very rough way, Milsark's binary strong/weak classification mirrors Ioup's hierarchy.

One type of NP that Ioup does not incorporate into her hierarchy is the bare NP, exemplified in English by bare plurals. As an initial rough characterization, bare plural NPs follow the pattern of NPs with weak determiners in being permissible in *there*-insertion sentences:

(10) There are spiders in my bed.

As far as the more particular scope preference of bare NPs is concerned, Carlson (1977b) notes that bare plurals tend to take narrow scope relative to other NPs or operators within the sentence:

(11) a. Everyone read books about slugs.
     b. Yella didn't find spiders in her bed.

The properties illustrated by the sentences in (10) and (11) lead to the conclusion that the bare plurals should be grouped with the weakly quantified NPs, and thus the bare plurals would fall into place on the right-hand (narrow scope) side of Ioup's hierarchy.

The correspondence between Ioup's hierarchy and Milsark's classification is explained by the syntactic description I have given of strong and

weak determiners. The wide scope preference of strong determiners follows from the fact that they are always presuppositional and therefore are
always raised by QR. The application of QR guarantees that they always
have the IP as their scope domain. Weak determiners differ from strong
quantifiers in that they can have a cardinal reading in which they are
bound within the VP by existential closure. Thus, weak determiners on
their cardinal reading have only the VP as their scope domain. Their
narrower scope preference thus results from the fact that their scope
domain is contained within the higher IP-level scope domain of the strong
quantifiers.[14]

3.2.5   Relative Scope: An Additional Reading

Differentiating presuppositional and cardinal interpretations of NPs in
terms of QR leads to a second consequence of the syntactic characterization of strong and weak determiners. This result concerns certain relative
scope phenomena that arise from the ambiguity of the weak determiners.
This ambiguity permits a recursive embedding of tripartite logical representations in multiply-quantified sentences, with the consequence that an
additional reading emerges, which is not expected from traditional analyses of relative scope.

   Most accounts of multiply-quantified sentences such as (12) discuss only
two readings, which are determined only by the relative scope of the
quantified NPs that results from the ordered application of QR to the two
quantified NPs.

(12) Every cellist played some variations.

In a syntactic account such as May 1977, these two readings can be
represented through different orderings of the application of QR, as
shown in (13).[15]

(13) a. [Every cellist]$_\alpha$ [Some variations]$_\beta$ α played β
       b. [Some variations]$_\beta$ [Every cellist]$_\alpha$ α played β

In (13a) the subject NP *every cellist* takes wider scope than the object NP
some variations. In (13b) this relationship is reversed, with the object NP
taking scope over the subject NP.

   In the account I have presented, *three* readings are expected for the
sentence in (12). Because of the ambiguity of weak determiners, there are
in fact two, rather than only one, narrow scope readings for the object NP
some variations:

(14) a. [Every$_x$ [cellist(x)] Some$_y$ [variations(y)] x played y]
    b. [Every$_x$ [cellist(x)] ∃$_y$ variations(y) ∧ x played y]
    c. [Some$_y$ [variations(y)] Every$_x$ [cellist(x)] x played y]

Since *some* is a weak quantifier, it can have either a presuppositional reading (in which a restrictive clause is formed) or a cardinal reading (the NP remains within the VP/nuclear scope), regardless of whether it takes wide or narrow scope with respect to the subject NP. The narrow scope, presuppositional reading is shown in (14a), and the cardinal reading is shown in (14b). The third reading is the one in which the object NP gets wider scope, and here of course it has a presuppositional reading, since it must raise to IP to take scope over the subject, which has a strong determiner and therefore cannot lower to VP.

The derivations of the readings result in recursive embedding of tripartite structures. That is, the nuclear scope of the outermost restrictive clause in both (14a) and (14c) contains an embedded restrictive clause and its nuclear scope. (14b) is the more familiar simple tripartite structure. These readings can all be derived straightforwardly by QR followed by tree splitting, which maps the LF representations into the Heim-style logical representations. In the case of (14a), the first step is to adjoin the object NP *some variations* to IP (to derive the presuppositional reading). Next, the subject NP is adjoined to the left of the object NP. This gives the post-QR LF representation:

(15) [$_{IP}$ every cellist$_x$ [$_{IP}$ some variations$_y$ [$_{IP}$ t$_x$ [$_{VP}$ t$_x$ played t$_y$]]]]

Tree splitting now applies to the adjunction structure and "peels off" the first IP layer, forming a restrictive clause containing *cellist(x)*:

(16) Every$_x$ [cellist(x)] [$_{IP}$ some variations$_y$ [$_{VP}$ x played y]]

Since there is still a layer of IP that has not yet been affected by tree splitting, this step is repeated, producing another restrictive clause embedded below the first:

(17) Every$_x$ [cellist(x)] Some$_y$ [variations(y)] [$_{VP}$ x played y]

The VP is then mapped into a nuclear scope, with the traces functioning as variables:[16]

(18) Every$_x$ [cellist(x)] Some$_y$ [variations(y)] x played y

The derivations of the remaining two readings proceed along similar lines. In the case of (14b), with the narrow scope, cardinal reading of the object NP, no recursive embedding of tripartite structures is necessary.

The wide scope reading of the object NP in (14c) produces an embedded structure by the recursive peeling off of IP layers just as in the derivation of (18). Thus, the relative scope interpretation of quantified NPs in multiply-quantified sentences involves the interaction of two factors that can to some extent vary independently: relative scope and presuppositionality.

3.2.6   Does the Third Reading Really Exist?

Incorporating the notion of presuppositionality into the account of the strong/weak distinction leads to the prediction that there are three, rather than the usual two, readings in a case of multiple quantification such as (12), repeated here:

(19) Every cellist played some variations.

The "extra" reading results from the ambiguity of weak quantifiers. Since weak quantifiers can have both cardinal and presuppositional readings, there are actually *two* possible narrow scope readings for the object NP *some variations*: a presuppositional reading (14a) and a cardinal reading (14b). The third reading for the sentence is that in which a wide scope reading obtains for the object NP. This third reading is, I think, uncontroversial. Less obvious may be the distinction between the two narrow scope readings for the object NP. The distinction between the cardinal and presuppositional narrow scope readings is subtle, but I think it can be brought out by presenting appropriate contexts for each of the readings.

Considering (19), one possible situation that would be common to all three readings is a competition for cellists. Each cellist plays some pieces, and the judges will pick the winner based on overall performance. When it comes to the variations, the competition could proceed in a number of different ways, allowing us to differentiate the three readings of (19). In the first case, there could be a list of optional pieces for the competition, including Tchaikovsky's Rococo Variations, Beethoven's Variations on a theme from "Judas Maccabeus," and Mendelssohn's Variations Concertantes. From this list each cellist picks a set of variations of his or her choice (they do not necessarily pick the same ones). In this context the sentence *Every cellist played some variations* exhibits the narrow scope, presuppositional reading for the object NP. This context involves selection of variations from a preestablished (or presupposed) set.

This contrasts with another possible scenario, in which there is no list of sets of variations. In fact, in this competition the cellists all must improvise a set of variations. It's not likely the cellists would end up playing the same variations, and as improvisations their existence could hardly be presupposed. This is the narrow scope cardinal reading for *some variations*.[17] The context for the wide scope reading is straightforward. All the cellists play some variations, and they all play the same variations, for example, perhaps Tchaikovsky's Rococo Variations.

Since numerals behave in the same manner as weak determiners, these three readings can also be distinguished when a numeral quantifier appears on the object NP:

(20) Every person saw three ghosts.

Here the basic context could be visiting an old, rundown house. On the narrow scope, presuppositional reading of *three ghosts* the house could be known to be haunted by a set of ghosts such as the ghosts of all of Bach's 20-odd children. In this context, every person could see three of the ghosts, the partitive *of* indicating the presuppositional reading.

On the cardinal reading, the house would have no such preestablished reputation. Every person could see three ghosts, even three different ghosts each time. In this case the sentence in (20) would merely assert the existence of ghosts seen. Finally, on the wide scope reading, three well-known ghosts could be seen by every member of the visiting party, such as the ghost of Tchaikovsky, the ghost of Salieri, and the ghost of Millard Fillmore.

Although the difference between the presuppositional reading and the cardinal reading of a narrow scope weak NP is subtle, it can be highlighted by the context chosen. This is of course not at all surprising, since the difference between the two readings hinges on what is or isn't presupposed in the conversation. We can therefore conclude that taking into account the strong/weak distinction in a syntactic derivation of relative scope leads to a more complete account of the available readings.

3.2.7 Overview of Quantified NP Interpretations

So far we have seen that the tree-splitting procedure developed here has a number of consequences for a theory of the interpretation of indefinites. One result is that it has become clear that indefinite NPs should in fact be treated as being ambiguous between a cardinal reading and a presuppositional reading. Furthermore, examination of Milsark's classification of determiners shows that this classification corresponds neatly to the reclassification of indefinites that is required by the implementation of the Mapping Hypothesis. Incorporating the notion of "presupposition accommodation" into the tree-splitting procedure leads to an explanation of Milsark's "semantic" distinction between strong and weak determiners in syntactic terms. Strong quantifiers adjoin to IP at LF (by QR); weak quantifiers remain within the domain of VP at LF. The cardinal/pre-suppositional contrast is thus represented in the logical representation by the presence or absence of a restrictive clause. The scope order differences between the two types of quantifiers (as observed by Ioup (1975)) result from their different domains at LF: IP and VP.

3.3   QR, Presuppositions, and the Mapping Hypothesis

In the discussion of the ambiguity of indefinites given above I claimed that there is a close connection between the more or less semantic notion of "presupposition of existence" and the application of the syntactic rule QR. To the extent that there is syntactic evidence for a syntactic rule of QR (such as that presented by May (1985)), there should also be syntactic reflexes of the ambiguity of indefinites. In the sections that follow I exam-ine this connection between syntax and interpretation more closely and show that there is indeed a close syntactic connection between the presup-positional nature of certain NPs and their ability to appear in particular constructions that require quantificational (e.g., QRed) NPs.

QR also predictably disambiguates the two readings of indefinites (that is, weak NPs). In this connection I explore in more detail the close rela-tionship between S-structure word order and the semantic interpretation of NPs in German that was introduced in chapter 2. I also examine the connection between the "outer" subject position ([Spec, IP]) and presup-positionality that is implied by the workings of the Mapping Hypothesis.

3.3.1   Antecedent-Contained Deletion: An Indicator of QR
One way to test the connection between quantifier raising and presupposi-tion is to look at constructions where QR is required as a condition for grammaticality. In such contexts those NPs that do not undergo QR should produce an ungrammatical result, contrasting with those that do undergo QR. Put in another way, these constructions should disallow cardinal interpretations of NPs. Recent work on the syntax of LF has revealed a promising candidate for such a diagnostic of quantifier raising. This construction is a particular instance of VP-deletion known as *ante-cedent-contained deletion* (Bouton 1970, Sag 1976, Williams 1977, May 1985).

To see why antecedent-contained deletion (ACD) requires QR, we must first consider the constraints that apply to VP-deletions in general. These constraints are outlined in the work of Williams and Sag. In particular, Sag (1976) claims that VP-deletion is subject to the c-command constraint given in (21).

(21) *C-command constraint on VP-deletion*
   VP-deletion is possible iff neither the missing verb (marked by *do*) nor its antecedent c-commands the other.

This c-command constraint is obviously satisfied in the case of VP-deletion in sentential conjunctions:

(22) a. Robert played piano and Clara did too.
     b. Robert played piano and Clara played piano too.

In (22a) neither the antecedent verb *played* nor the verb *did* (which marks the deletion site) c-commands the other, and as a result the sentence is grammatical. The deletion can also be easily recovered (following Williams (1977)) by simply copying the antecedent in the place of the deletion, as shown in (22b). Since the c-command constraint is satisfied, VP-deletion can apply freely in these cases of conjunction, with no restrictions on the form or interpretation (such as obligatory quantifier raising) of the object NP.

ACDs, on the other hand, are a special case of VP-deletion that appear to violate the c-command condition, a fact that was also noted by May (1985):

(23) Robert played every piano that Clara did.

In (23) the antecedent verb *played* c-commands the site of deletion (indicated by *did*), violating the c-command constraint. Reconstitution of the deletion by direct copying of the antecedent is also impossible, since it leads to an infinite regress because the antecedent actually contains the deletion. But in spite of this apparent violation of the c-command constraint, the fact remains that the sentence is grammatical.

Both Sag (1976) and Williams (1977) have used the problem of ACD as a basis for arguing that the constraints on VP-deletion should apply to some abstract syntactic level of logical representation (e.g., LF), rather than to S-structure. The effect of this refinement of the constraints on VP-deletion is clearly seen in cases that involve the application of QR. For example, in the case of (23), stating the constraints on VP-deletion at LF means that the c-command constraint in (21) applies to the structure after QR has applied (May 1985):

(24) a. [$_{IP}$ Robert [$_{VP}$ played [$_{NP}$ every piano that Clara [$_{VP}$ e]]]]

b. [[$_{NP}$ every piano that Clara [e]]$_i$ [Robert played [$_{NP}$ t$_i$]]]

c. [[every piano that Clara played [$_{NP}$ t$_i$]] [Robert played [$_{NP}$ t$_i$]]]

As May notes, the application of QR to the structure in (24a), shown in (24b), yields a structure in which the c-command constraint is no longer violated. After the object NP (which contains the deletion site) is adjoined to IP, neither the antecedent verb nor the deletion site c-commands the other. Recovery of the deletion is also now possible, since copying the antecedent (which is now the trace left by QR) no longer produces an infinite regress, as shown in (24c). Thus, to borrow May's apt description, QR licenses ACD by "disentangling" the infinite regress that it produces.

ACDs can therefore be thought of as a diagnostic for QR. ACD is grammatical only when the deletion is contained within an NP that undergoes QR. This leads to the prediction that if the deletion is not contained within an NP that undergoes QR (such as a cardinal indefinite bound by existential closure), ACD will be produce an ungrammatical results. As a consequence, ACD should distinguish between cardinal and presuppositional indefinites. Therefore, it is not surprising that Carlson (1977a) notes that ACD contexts require a noncardinal NP ((25d) and (26e) are Carlson's examples):[18]

(25) a. I read every book that you did.
b. I read each book that you did.
c. I read most books that you did.
d. Max put everything he could in his pockets.

(26) a. *?I read many books that you did.
b. *I read few books that you did.
c. *I read two books that you did.
d. *I read books that you did.
e. *Max put some/many/six things he could in his pockets.

The sentences in (25) are fine in any context. The sentences in (26) are unquestionably ungrammatical in the case of the cardinal (nonpartitive) reading.[19] Since QR "saves" ACDs from violating Sag's c-command constraint, those cases where ACD is not grammatical must be those where QR does not take place. The examples in (25) and (26) show that this correlation is paralleled by the strong/weak distinction. Thus, the contrast in grammaticality between (25) and (26) indicates that there is indeed a contrast between the strong and weak quantifiers with respect to whether or not they induce the application of QR.[20]

The story is not quite so simple as saying that strong quantifiers induce QR and weak quantifiers don't, however. Since the weak determiners are in fact ambiguous, whether or not an NP is raised by QR depends on more than just the choice of determiner. Presupposition is the deciding factor. In contexts that are unambiguously presuppositional, weak determiners like *many* and *two* can appear with NPs containing a deletion. This is illustrated by the following examples containing partitive (and therefore presuppositional) NPs with weak determiners:

(27) a. *There are two of the cows in the stable.

   b. *There are many of the pianos in need of tuning.

(28) a. I read two of the books that you did.

   b. Robert played many of the pianos that Clara did.

The sentences in (27) show that NPs such as *two of the books* function as strong, or presuppositional, NPs in that they cannot appear in *there*-insertion sentences. (28) shows that ACD is fine with NPs of this type, indicating that QR has occurred. Thus, it is not merely the choice of the determiner that determines whether QR takes place; the context must induce a presuppositional reading for the NP.

In summary, using the context of ACD as a diagnostic for QR allows for the testing of claims concerning the conditions for application of QR. The examples that I have considered show that there is a contrast between strong and weak determiners with respect to QR, just as would be expected under the analysis of NP interpretation proposed here. In addition, the contrast between presuppositional NPs and nonpresuppositional NPs in ACD contexts shows that the relevant factor in inducing QR is in fact presupposition, regardless of the choice of determiner.

3.3.2 Antecedent-Contained Deletion versus Extraposition

The discussion in the previous section relies crucially on the quantifier-raising analysis of ACD proposed by May (1985). This analysis is not uncontroversial, however. In this section I examine a number of objections to the ACD analysis raised by Baltin (1987). I conclude that Baltin's proposed alternative analysis is in fact inferior to the QR analysis in that it does not adequately account for the distribution of ACD, nor does it explain the close relationship between presuppositional interpretations and the acceptability of ACDs.

Although May's analysis (as well as those of Sag (1976) and Williams (1977)) resolves the problem of recovering ACDs by means of an abstract intermediate level (LF) at which the deleted VP is no longer contained in its antecedent, Baltin (1987) claims that the relevant level for reconstitution of the deleted VP is S-structure. Since Baltin assumes in this connection that the c-command constraint proposed by Sag is correct, his proposal amounts to the claim that ACD is in fact never possible. In the face of this apparent contradiction, Baltin claims that apparent ACDs are actually just cases of string-vacuous extraposition at S-structure, rather than involving movement (e.g., QR) at the abstract level of LF. In other words, apparent ACD sentences are derived in a fashion parallel to cases of PP- and S'-extraposition (discussed in Ross 1967, Guéron 1980, Baltin 1981, 1984, and Guéron and May 1984, among others). Examples are given in (29) and (30).

(29) a. A man who was from Bisbee arrived.
     b. A man arrived who was from Bisbee.

(30) a. A review of "Jabberwocky" arrived.
     b. A review arrived of "Jabberwocky."

In (29b) the relative clause *who was from Bisbee* is extraposed, and in (30b) the PP *of "Jabberwocky"* is extraposed.

In Baltin's analysis, this process is extended to the apparent ACDs, so that the sentence in (31) involves string-vacuous extraposition of the relative clause *that Clara did*. The relative clause adjoins to VP at S-structure, resulting in a structure in which the deletion site is no longer contained in its antecedent.

(31) Robert played every piano that Clara did.

The result of this extraposition is shown in the tree in (32). The structural relationship between the extraposed clause and its antecedent is illustrated by the boxes outlining the two parts.

(32) *Baltin's extraposition analysis of ACD*

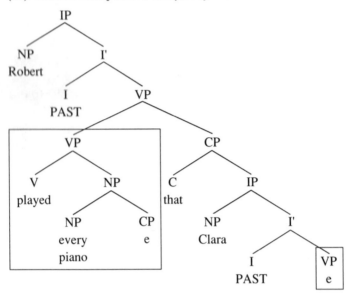

The smaller box outlines the deletion site, and the larger box outlines the antecedent VP. As a result of the extraposition operation, the "deletion box" is no longer contained within the "antecedent box." Thus, in Baltin's analysis ACDs do not create problems with regard to the application of Sag's c-command constraint simply because ACDs do not exist at S-structure.[21]

If Baltin's analysis is correct, then ACD sentences might not in fact be indicators of QR. In his account the acceptability of (31) has nothing to do with LF movement of the NP *every piano ...*; therefore, QR is not relevant. It is not clear that this analysis is correct, however. In response to Baltin's analysis, Larson and May (1990) point out that ACDs differ internally from extraposed relatives and therefore should not be given an extraposition analysis. In addition to their arguments (involving the form and position of the subordinate clause and the interpretation of the deleted VP), I present some additional differences between extraposition structures and ACD that provide further evidence in support of the QR analysis.

If the apparent ACD structures are actually derived by extraposition, ACD and the other extraposition structures should be subject to the same restrictions. There does not seem to be a parallelism between the two types of constructions, however. Free relatives are one case of a syntactic environment in which extraposition and ACD clearly show different behavior. Extraposition is impossible with free relatives (McCawley 1988: 432), whereas ACDs occur quite freely:[22]

(33) a. *It's still in the car what he bought.
     b. *It needs tuning whatever piano Clara played.

(34) a. Robert played whatever piano Clara did.
     b. I read whatever books you did.

Thus, extraposition and ACD show a rather different distribution with respect to free relatives. This fact gives an initial indication that ACDs cannot satisfactorily be given an extraposition-based analysis.

An even more striking difference between ACDs and extraposition structures involves the requirements imposed on the determiner of the NP involved. As I noted earlier, ACD requires a strong, or presuppositional, determiner:

(35) a. *I read books that you did.
     b. *I read two books that you did.

(36) a. I read every book that you did.
     b. I read each book that you did.

This is not true of PP-extraposition or relative clause extraposition. In fact, nonvacuous cases of extraposition from NPs with strong determiners are significantly less acceptable than the comparable cases involving weak determiners (see Guéron 1981 and Reinhart 1987):[23]

(37) a. *Olga sent every person to the library who wanted books on obscure Prussian composers.
     b. *Most men arrived who were from Bisbee.
     c. *Oscar gave each spider to Otto that was poisonous.
     d. Olga sent every person who wanted books on obscure Prussian composers to the library.
     e. Most men who were from Bisbee arrived.
     f. Oscar gave each spider that was poisonous to Otto.

(38) a. *Every review appeared of "Jabberwocky."
     b. *Each review appeared of this outrageous opera.
     c. Every review of "Jabberwocky" appeared.
     d. Each review of this outrageous opera appeared.

In (37) and (38) the examples involving extraposition from strong NPs are all ungrammatical, whereas the unextraposed versions are fine.

Thus, the most usual cases of extraposition do not show the property that is most essential to the quantifier-raising analysis of ACD structures: being licensed by a determiner that induces QR. In fact, they impose exactly the opposite restriction in that they require cardinal NPs. Regardless of the explanation of the judgments in (37) and (38), the fact that the ACD structures discussed in the previous section require presuppositional NPs and the extraposition structures in (37) and (38) require cardinal NPs strongly indicates that they should be given different analyses. As for the constraints on extraposition, I will discuss constraints on extraction from NPs in chapter 4, and some of these arguments may extend to the extraposition cases.

The comparison of the syntactic constraints imposed on ACD and extraposition shows that they should not be given the same analysis. Therefore, I will continue to assume that May's (1985) QR analysis of ACD is essentially correct and that as a consequence of this analysis, ACD structures act as a diagnostic for QR.[24]

3.3.3   VP-Deletion and the Mapping Hypothesis

In presenting and justifying the Mapping Hypothesis, so far I have allowed myself two simplifications: I have limited my discussion of quantifier raising to the case of adjunction to IP, and I have described the tree-splitting procedure somewhat vaguely, in terms of largely intuitive notions of VP-internal versus VP-external. In this section I discuss some data that seem to require expanding the range of the rule of QR. This in turn leads to a reexamination of the tree-splitting procedure in order to make the notions of "material inside the VP" and "material outside the VP" more explicit.

Although adjunction to IP is often presented as the central case of QR, a number of researchers have proposed that QR should be more general in that quantifier phrases should be able to adjoin to nodes other than IP (Williams 1977, Stowell 1981, DeCarrico 1983, May 1985). One argument in favor of quantifier raising to VP in particular is based on facts concerning the interaction of quantifier scope with VP-deletion noted by Sag (1976) and Williams (1977).[25]

Williams and Sag both note that multiply-quantified sentences are generally ambiguous in isolation, but in the context of VP-deletion the ambiguity disappears, and only the scope order corresponding to the linear order of the quantified NPs is possible:[26]

(39) a. Some bassoonist played every sonata.

     b. Some bassoonist played every sonata, but Otto didn't.

Thus, in (39a) the object NP *every sonata* can take either wide or narrow scope with respect to the subject NP *some bassoonist*. In (39b) only the narrow scope reading for the object NP is possible. The reason for this is said to be that reconstructing (at the level of LF) a VP containing the NP *every sonata* and the variable it binds will yield a well-formed logical representation (40a). If the object NP is raised to IP for the wide scope reading, an unbound variable will result when the VP is reconstructed, as shown in (40b).

(40) a. $[_{IP}$ some bassoonist$_j$ $[_{IP}$ t$_j$ $[_{VP}$ every sonata$_i$ $[_{VP}$ played t$_i]]]]$
  and Otto didn't $[_{VP}$ every sonata$_i$ $[_{VP}$ played t$_i]]$
  b. $[_{IP}$ every sonata$_i$ $[_{IP}$ some bassoonist$_j$ $[_{IP}$ t$_j$ $[_{VP}$ played t$_i]]]]$
  and Otto didn't $[_{VP}$ played t$_i]$

In (40b) the second occurrence of t_i is left unbound, since it is outside the scope of *every sonata*, which is limited to the first conjunct.

The account of quantifier scope that I have developed so far makes two claims. First, the domain of existential closure is the VP; and second, NPs that are outside VP at the point of tree splitting are mapped into restrictive clause structures. I have not defined what constitutes being "inside" or "outside" the VP, relying only on purely intuitive notions of containment and inclusion. The VP-deletion facts indicate that some more careful explication of the tree-splitting procedure is necessary. One particular question to be answered is this: Is quantifier adjunction to VP ruled out by the Mapping Hypothesis? To answer this question, we need to specify more explicitly what is "inside the VP" in the context of adjunction, since it is clear that we do not want to map QRed phrases such as the NP *every sonata* in (40b) into the nuclear scope of the logical representation.

May (1985) and Chomsky (1986a) discuss adjunction structures and the formal problems they raise with respect to relationships such as domination and containment, or inclusion. Both May and Chomsky assume that in an adjunction structure the category adjoined to a maximal projection is neither dominated by, nor included in, that projection. Adjunction thus creates a projection consisting of "segments," and the resulting segmented projection dominates only those categories that are dominated by *all* segments of the projection. This leads to a precise definition of the concept of *inclusion* in terms of this revised conception of dominance:

(41) α *includes* β if and only if β is dominated by every segment of α.

Thus, in (40b) the VP-adjoined quantifier phrase is not included in the VP. If the informal characterization "inside the VP" is defined as "included in

VP," then adjunction to VP will not create any problems with regard
to correctly forming the nuclear scope of the logical representation. Additionally, the notion "outside the VP" can be correspondingly clarified as
"not included in VP," allowing for the correct correspondence with restrictive clause formation.[27] The answer to the question concerning VP-
adjunction of quantifiers is that quantifier raising to VP is possible (and
needed) within the theory of quantifier interpretation I have developed
here, and the Sag-Williams-May analysis of the contrast in (39) can be
retained.[28]

3.3.4 The Ambiguity of Weak Quantifiers in German

The syntactic account of the cardinal/presuppositional contrast that I
have proposed carries with it the obvious implication that there is a close
connection between the [Spec, IP] position (or anything not included in
VP, in the case of adjunction) and presuppositional NPs. In this section I
will look more closely at this connection, drawing on data from German.

   The close connection between the [Spec, IP] position and presuppositional NPs predicts a close relation between the position of the subject and
the ambiguity of weak determiners. In other words, the position of the
subject should affect the interpretation of an NP with a weak quantifier.
In English this correlation between subject position and interpretation
is obscured by the fact that all subjects must appear in [Spec, IP] at
S-structure. The alternation of interpretations and subject positions can
only appear at the abstract level of LF (after LF lowering can apply). The
fact that subjects can appear in either of the two positions at S-structure in
German ([Spec, IP] and [Spec, VP]), coupled with the fact that tree splitting can reflect S-structure word order in German (as was shown by the
bare plural facts presented in chapter 2), predicts that there should be an
alternation between the cardinal and presuppositional readings of a weak
determiner on a subject NP depending on the S-structure position of the
NP.

   In the following examples I show a case where the position of the subject
alternates with respect to sentential particles, similar to the case I discussed
in chapter 2 with respect to bare plural subjects. Recall that sentential
particles can appear either to the left or to the right of the subject NP:

(42) a. ... weil ja doch zwei Cellisten in diesem Hotel abgestiegen sind.
              since 'indeed' two cellists in this   hotel have-taken-rooms
      b. ... weil zwei Cellisten ja doch in diesem Hotel abgestiegen sind.
              since two cellists   'indeed' in this   hotel have-taken-rooms

presupp. reading   Cardinal reading. Spec VP.
Spec IP.
2 of some larger set of cellists

I will assume that when the subject appears to the right of the particles it is in [Spec, VP], and when it appears to the left of the particles it is in [Spec, IP], as I argued in chapter 2. Thus, the particles serve to diagnose the position of the subject. Varying the position of the subject in this way does in fact lead to an alternation in the interpretation of the subject NP *zwei Cellisten* 'two cellists'. In (42a), with the subject NP in [Spec, VP], the cardinal reading is most salient. The sentence in (42a) asserts the existence of two cellists who have taken rooms in this hotel. This is not unexpected, since the tree-splitting algorithm will map the subject occupying the [Spec, VP] position into the nuclear scope of the logical representation, giving rise to the existential, or cardinal, reading.

In (42b), on the other hand, the subject NP is in [Spec, IP]. Here the presuppositional reading obtains. In this case the two cellists are two of some larger set of cellists. The context situation might be one in which a busload of cellists has arrived in town (perhaps for a Villa-Lobos festival), and two of the cellists are staying in this hotel, four more at a local bed-and-breakfast, another with an aunt, and so on.[29] The presuppositional reading is thus associated with the outer, [Spec, IP] subject position. Again, this is not a surprising result, given the workings of the Mapping Hypothesis. The indefinite subject in [Spec, IP] is mapped into a restrictive clause by tree splitting. This restrictive clause represents the existential presupposition of the subject NP, resulting in the contrast in interpretation between (42a) and (42b).[30]

Summarizing the results of the preceding subsections: I presented a variety of evidence in support of the syntactic account of the cardinal/presuppositional contrast that I proposed in the beginning of this chapter. The association of presuppositionality with restrictive clause formation via the operation of tree splitting predicts that there should be a close connection between presuppositionality and quantifier raising, which involves adjunction to IP. This prediction was borne out by the case of ACD constructions in English, in which grammaticality depends on the application of QR. The relationship between restrictive clause formation and the presuppositional interpretation of indefinites also suggests that there should be a connection between [Spec, IP] and presuppositional readings of indefinites. The German data concerning the interpretation of indefinite subjects show that there is in fact a contrast between [Spec, IP] and [Spec, VP] with respect to the interpretation of indefinites.

3.4   Dutch Subjects, Turkish Objects, and "Specificity"

So far in this chapter I have focused on the existence of two particular readings for indefinites, a cardinal (existential closure) reading and a presuppositional or quantificational reading. In this section I extend my treatment of presupposition and the interpretation of indefinites to a number of semantico-syntactic phenomena that have been described in terms of the notion of "specificity." The data concerned are from Dutch and Turkish and have been described and analyzed by Reuland (1988) and Enç (1991).

The exact nature of specificity has been the subject of some debate. An initial point of controversy concerns whether specificity is actually a semantic notion (as suggested by Donnellan (1966) and others) or whether it is more properly treated as a matter of pragmatics (as suggested by Kripke (1977) and also Ludlow and Neale (1991)). My approach here will be from the viewpoint of the interactions between the syntax and specific interpretations of NPs. Since specificity does in fact correlate with a number of syntactic phenomena such as word order and case marking in a number of languages, it is reasonable to take the semantic approach to specificity, since syntactic effects might be unexpected under an account in terms of pragmatics. Additionally, any semantic account of specificity will have to explicate how the connection to the syntactic reflexes of specificity is to be made, or how specificity is to be represented in the mapping from syntax to semantics.[31]

In the following sections I will reexamine some cases of specificity presented by Reuland and Enç and show that they can be nicely accommodated into the account of presuppositionality and quantifier raising that I have developed in this chapter. In other words, the various facts described by Reuland and Enç can be explained by regarding the essential semantic contribution of "specificity" as being in fact presuppositionality. This approach has the very interesting result that the concomitant syntactic reflexes of specificity, such as word order in Dutch and case marking in Turkish (which remain mysterious on purely semantic or pragmatic accounts of specificity), end up being explained by the syntactic connection between presuppositionality and restrictive clause formation effected by the tree-splitting procedure.

3.4.1   Dutch Indefinite Subjects
Indefinite subjects in Dutch have a number of interesting syntactic and semantic properties (see Kerstens 197S, De Haan 1979, Bennis 1986,

Reuland 1988, and Rullmann 1989). Before considering the data regarding what have been called "specific" NPs, I will present some more basic facts concerning the interpretation of indefinite subjects in Dutch. These facts have been discussed by a number of researchers, as noted in the references given above. Though I take most of the examples in this section from Reuland 1988, I believe most (if not all) of the descriptive generalizations presented below can be attributed to the other authors as well (although the theoretical explanations of course vary).

As in German, the interpretation of bare plural subjects in Dutch varies with their syntactic position. In particular, Reuland notes the following paradigm concerning the syntax and semantics of bare plural subjects in Dutch:

(43) a. *Fred denkt dat koeien op het dak liggen.
       Fred thinks that cows on the roof lie
   b. Fred denkt dat er   koeien op het dak liggen.
       Fred thinks that there cows   on the roof lie
       'Fred thinks that there are cows lying on the roof.'
   c. Fred denkt dat koeien lui zijn.
       Fred thinks that cows   lazy are
       'Fred thinks that cows are lazy.'

Looking only at the embedded clause portions of the sentences in (43) (I restrict myself to embedded clauses in order to avoid the complications brought about by the verb-second constraint in Dutch), we can see that there is a contrast in the acceptability of the bare plural subject *koeien* 'cows'. (43a) shows that the bare plural subject is ungrammatical in the initial position of an embedded clause with a locative predicate. This contrasts with (43b), in which the bare plural subject in the embedded clause is immediately preceded by an expletive *er* 'there'. In this case the sentence is grammatical, and the bare plural has an existential interpretation. Finally, (43c) shows that a clause-initial bare plural subject is grammatical in the case of a predicate denoting a more or less permanent state such as *lui* 'lazy'. Not surprisingly, in this context the sentence is interpreted as a generic statement about cows.[32]

In considering the derivation of the logical representations of the sentences in (43), I will follow Reuland in assuming that the [Spec, IP] position *cannot* be empty at S-structure in Dutch (that is, Dutch does not permit null expletives). I will also assume that Dutch is like German in that the tree-splitting operation must occur at S-structure (or, stated differently, indefinite subjects cannot undergo LF lowering in Dutch). Given these assumptions, the logical representations of the embedded clauses in (43) are as follows:

(44) a. *Gen_x [x is a cow] x is on the roof
   b. [er] $\exists_x$ x is a cow $\wedge$ x is on the roof
   c. Gen_x [x is a cow] x is lazy

The representation in (44a) corresponds to the ungrammatical sentence in (43a). In this case the bare plural subject, which must be in [Spec, IP] since it appears leftmost in the clause, is mapped into a restrictive clause, where it is then bound by the generic operator *Gen* (see Wilkinson 1986, Gerstner and Krifka 1987, and the discussion in chapter 2 of this monograph). This leads to a generic interpretation of the subject. However, this generic interpretation is pragmatically incompatible with the locative predicate 'on-the-roof', leading to the judgment of ungrammaticality seen in (43a).[33]

In (43b) the [Spec, IP] position is filled at S-structure by the expletive *er* 'there'. The lexical subject *koeien* 'cows' thereby occupies the VP-internal subject position. Tree splitting in this case maps the bare plural subject 'cows' into the nuclear scope, and the restrictive clause is filled by the expletive, which may function as a "locative presupposition" (see Bennis 1986). This yields an existential reading for the bare plural subject, since it is in this case bound by existential closure (see (44b)). This existential reading is compatible with the locative predicate; therefore, unlike (43a), (43b) is grammatical.

Finally, in (43c) the bare plural subject is in the external subject position [Spec, IP], as in (43a). The subject is mapped by the tree-splitting procedure into a restrictive clause, where it is bound by the generic operator to yield the generic reading, as shown in (44c). But unlike the case of (43a), the generic reading of the subject is quite compatible with the individual-level predicate 'is-lazy'.

Thus, the contrasts in interpretation noted in (43) are explained by the Mapping Hypothesis plus two additional assumptions: the [Spec, IP] position cannot be empty in Dutch, and tree splitting occurs at S-structure in Dutch. Thus, when no NP or PP fills the [Spec, IP] position, it is filled by the expletive *er*. In this case the (lexical) subject appears in the VP-internal subject position. As a result of the tree-splitting algorithm, this syntactic fact about Dutch leads to a peculiar semantic property of indefinite subjects in that language. Indefinite subjects in the clause-initial ([Spec, IP]) position must be interpreted as forming a restrictive clause, and they will only be grammatical in those cases where such an interpretation is plausible.

This direct association between the [Spec, IP] position and the restrictive clause interpretation of a bare plural subject (as opposed to the VP-internal existential closure interpretation) leads to the expectation that a similar contrast in interpretation should arise with other indefinite subjects (in addition to the bare plural). Turning now to subjects with weak quantifiers (which in English are ambiguous between the restrictive clause and existential closure interpretations), we see the following difference in interpretation with respect to the S-structure position of the subject (again, these examples are adapted from Reuland 1988, but similar examples are also found in Kerstens 1975):

(45) a. Fred denkt dat [$_{IP}$ twee koeien op het dak liggen].
　　　 Fred thinks that 　　 two cows 　 on the roof lie
　　　 'Fred thinks that two (specific) cows are lying on the roof.'
　 b. Fred denkt dat [$_{IP}$ er 　 [$_{VP}$ twee koeien op het dak liggen]].
　　　 Fred thinks that 　 there 　 two cows 　 on the roof lie
　　　 'Fred thinks that there are two cows lying on the roof.'

The sentences in (45) are identical except that in (45a) the embedded subject NP *twee koeien* 'two cows' appears in [Spec, IP], whereas in (45b) [Spec, IP] is occupied by *er* 'there', and the lexical subject NP is in the VP-internal subject position [Spec, VP]. Reuland claims that the subject NPs in the two sentences differ in interpretation. In (45a), with the external subject, no existential reading is possible. The only possible reading is what Reuland calls a "specific" reading. In (45b), with the subject in the VP-internal position, the subject NP has an existential reading.

The examples in (45) show that the VP-internal subject position is associated with an existential reading. This is not at all surprising given the discussion so far. A VP-internal subject maps into the nuclear scope, where it is bound by existential closure. What remains to be determined is the exact nature of the "specific" reading that Reuland associates with the subject NP in the VP-external subject position. By analogy to the bare plural examples, we would expect that the VP-external interpretation would show properties characteristic of restrictive clause formation. Rullmann (1989) provides the empirical evidence needed to make this connection. Rullmann's examples show that the nature of specificity becomes quite clear when these "specific" NPs are placed in appropriate discourse contexts that highlight the relevant semantic property involved. One of Rullmann's examples is given in (46).[34]

(46) Toen ik de bibliotheek in wilde gaan werd de ingang geblokkeerd
door een groep studenten.
'When I wanted to enter the library, the entrance was blocked by a
group of students.'

Ik hoorde later dat *twee studenten* gearresteerd waren.
I   heard   later   that   students   arrested   were
'Later I heard that two (of the) students had been arrested.'

The second sentence in the discourse given in (46) contains an indefinite
subject NP, *twee studenten* 'two students', in the embedded clause. The
absence of an expletive *er* to the left of the subject indicates that the
subject occupies the [Spec, IP] position. In the context provided by the
preceding sentence, the subject NP *twee studenten* must have a partitive
reading in which the two students are two of those previously mentioned
that blocked the library entrance. (Rullmann calls these examples "concealed partitives.") In my earlier discussion of the ambiguity of indefinites
I claimed that paraphrasability as a partitive is one indicator of the property that I have called presuppositionality. If this is the case, then Rullmann's "concealed partitives" show that the "specific" reading observed
by Reuland actually involves the notion of presupposition.[35] The specific
indefinites in these examples are indefinites that receive a presuppositional,
restrictive clause interpretation in which the determiner functions as an
operator (it has quantificational force of its own). The nonspecific indefinites are existential closure indefinites. These NPs have no quantificational force, and their determiners function as cardinality predicates.[36]

This approach to the specificity contrast in Dutch indefinite subjects is
further supported by the syntactic nature of the contrast—it is the syntactic positioning of the subject that yields the contrast. The parallel between
Reuland's observations and the syntax of weak determiner ambiguity
becomes clear. The weak NP *twee studenten* in [Spec, IP] is presuppositional, as indicated by its "partitive" interpretation. Its presuppositional
interpretation is semantically represented by the subject being mapped
into a restrictive clause in the logical representation (which is in fact
required by the Mapping Hypothesis). When the subject NP is in [Spec,
VP], as in (45b), it can only have an existential interpretation. This is again
expected given the Mapping Hypothesis, which maps the VP-internal
subject into the nuclear scope of the logical representation, yielding only
the existential reading. Thus, Reuland's examples can be regarded as
somewhat parallel to the German examples involving the ambiguity of
weak determiners given in section 3.3.4.

In conclusion, the presuppositionality of indefinite subject NPs is syntactically marked in Dutch. Presuppositional subject NPs appear in the outer, [Spec, IP] position, and nonpresuppositional, or cardinal, subject NPs appear in the inner, [Spec, VP] position. This supports the Mapping Hypothesis in that the notion of presupposition and restrictive clause formation is shown to be linked to the [Spec, IP] position. The connection between [Spec, IP] and presupposition is made by the tree-splitting procedure, which maps indefinites at the IP level into restricted quantifier structures. This approach also explains two commonly noted aspects of the "specific" reading of indefinite subjects in Dutch: its semantic relation to "partitive" NPs, and its syntactic association with the [Spec, IP] subject position.

3.4.2 Turkish Objects

There are other syntactic mechanisms that languages can make use of to mark the presuppositionality (or lack thereof) of an NP. In this section I consider an instance of syntactic marking of presuppositional NPs from Turkish (based on data from Enç 1991). Unlike the case of Dutch subjects, in which the presuppositional reading was marked by placement of the indefinite NP clearly outside of the VP, the presuppositionality of the Turkish NPs is marked, not by their syntactic position, but by morphological case marking.

In Turkish, object NPs may or may not be morphologically marked for case. In particular, object NPs may appear either with the accusative case marker suffix -yi, or they may be bare, with no morphological case marking at all. What is interesting about this optionality of case marking is that it has semantic effects. Enç (1991) observes that the presence or absence of the accusative case marker produces a corresponding alternation in the semantic interpretation of the object NP, with the notion of "specificity" once again coming into play. To illustrate this effect, I give the examples in (47), with Enç's translations.

(47) a. Ali bir kitab-i   aldi.
        Ali one book-ACC bought
        'A book is such that Ali bought it.'
     b. Ali bir kitap aldi.
        Ali one book bought
        'Ali bought some book or other.'

In (47a) the object NP *kitab* 'book' is marked with accusative case. In this sentence the object NP can have only what Enç calls a "specific" reading. In (47b) there is no case marker on the object NP, and in this case the object has a nonspecific, or existential, reading. Thus, Enç claims that Turkish indefinite objects are not ambiguous between specific and non-specific interpretations (as English indefinites are), but are in fact disambiguated by the presence or absence of the accusative case marker.[37]

Although the syntactic mechanism involved in disambiguation is clearly different, this semantic alternation of a "specific" and an existential reading of object NPs looks rather like Reuland's description of the facts concerning the interpretation of Dutch subjects. And once again, these examples raise the question of what it means for an NP to be specific in this sense. Enç discusses the nature of specificity and reaches the conclusion that specificity must be described in terms of a feature [±specific] (represented as an additional index indicating definiteness). NPs that are marked [+specific] (such as object NPs bearing morphological case marking) must satisfy a Familiarity Condition, which basically requires that there be a discourse referent corresponding to the [+specific] indefinite (the Familiarity Condition is based on ideas in Heim 1982).

At this point it is not yet clear how this analysis of the "specific" reading should be related to the sorts of interpretations of indefinites developed here. Enç gives some additional data, however, that suggest that the account of "specificity" in these contexts could in fact be developed in terms of the analysis of indefinites that I have been developing here. In illustrating the difference between the two readings ([±specific]), Enç introduces sentences embedded in a discourse. Not surprisingly, these contexts look very much like Rullmann's "concealed partitives":

(48) a. Odam-a   birkaç çocuk girdi.
        my-room-DAT several child entered
        'Several children entered my room.'
     b. Iki kiz-i   tanıyordum.
        two girl-ACC I-knew
        'I knew two girls.'
     c. Iki kiz tanıyordum.
        two girl I-knew
        'I knew two girls.'

In the context that is established by (48a), either (48b) (with accusative case marking on the object NP) or (48c) (no morphological case on the object NP) can follow. The difference in case marking corresponds to a difference in interpretation. In the case of the accusative-marked NP, the two girls must be two of the girls who entered the room. If no case marker appears on the object NP, as in (48c), the two girls are two *additional* girls. Thus, the accusative case marking induces a concealed partitive reading for the object NP. In other words, the "specific" reading once again involves the notion of presupposition in that the "specificity" signaled by the accusative case marking corresponds directly to the formation of a restrictive clause that represents the set introduced in the preceding discourse.

As further evidence in support of this approach to the Turkish facts, it is interesting to note that object NPs that have unambiguously strong (or presuppositional) determiners also require the morphological accusative marker:

(49) a.   Ali her   kitab-i   okudu.
            Ali every book-ACC read
            'Ali read every book.'
      b.   *Ali her kitap okudu.

Thus, the generalization that emerges from the data is that presuppositional object NPs are distinguished from nonpresuppositional objects in that they must be morphologically marked with accusative case. Consequently, object NPs with weak determiners (that is, determiners that are in principle ambiguous between presuppositional and cardinal (existential) readings) receive accusative case marking only in presuppositional contexts such as that illustrated in (48).[38]

The Turkish facts provide another illustration of the fact that "specificity" in indefinites can be assimilated to the properties of the presuppositional readings that I have discussed above. As illustrated by both the Dutch and Turkish facts, the primary distinguishing property between specific and nonspecific indefinites is restrictive clause formation, in correspondence to the treatment of the ambiguity of indefinites given in section 3.2.3.

Turkish is also like Dutch in that the presuppositionality of NPs is syntactically marked. Whereas in Dutch this property is indicated positionally within the clause, in Turkish it is marked by the presence or absence of the accusative case marker. This raises the question of how the Turkish facts can be related to the Mapping Hypothesis. The problem is that accusative case marking (presumably a VP-internal process) correlates with restrictive clause formation, whereas the Mapping Hypothesis associates restrictive clause formation with NPs that are VP-external. There are two possible ways of approaching this dilemma.

The first approach simply calls into question the VP-internal nature of accusative case marking, following the lines of recent research in the framework of the expanded phrase structure of Pollock (1989) in which Infl is "exploded" into a number of functional heads. A number of researchers (see Van den Wyngaerd 1989 and Mahajan 1990, among others) have suggested that object NPs can actually move at S-structure out of the VP to the specifier of a functional head (e.g., [Spec, AgrO], following Chomsky (1991)) in order to receive accusative case. On this approach the presence of morphological case marking would actually signal a VP-*external* object, which would naturally be mapped into a restrictive clause by the Mapping Hypothesis. On this approach Turkish would be rather like German and Dutch in that the S-structure representation would map quite directly into the logical representations.

Another possibility is to simply assume that the accusative case marker in Turkish acts as an S-structure trigger for LF movement (e.g., QR) of an object NP. Object NPs that are not marked with accusative case do not trigger QR and therefore can receive only the VP-internal existential closure interpretation.[39] I will leave this issue open for now; it is not clear that much hinges on the choice taken at this point. In the next chapter I examine the interpretation of indefinite objects in English and German in more detail. In the case of German in particular the role of S-structure scrambling of NPs in determining semantic interpretation may be relevant to the ultimate choice of explanation for the Turkish data.

3.5   Some Final Remarks on the Nature of Specificity

The characterization of "specific" indefinites as being presuppositional, and therefore essentially quantificational, runs afoul of claims made by Fodor and Sag (1982) to the effect that specific indefinites show certain properties that preclude a quantificational analysis. Among the properties that Fodor and Sag demonstrate as evidence for a referential rather than quantificational analysis of indefinites are (1) the ability of indefinites to escape "scope islands," (2) the absence of certain "intermediate" scope readings with specific indefinites, and (3) the ability of specific indefinites (unlike other quantifiers) to appear in weak crossover configurations. I will deal with the weak crossover data in chapter 4, so I will confine myself here to commenting briefly on the other two properties. I also will not consider in any detail arguments concerning the viability of a referential analysis of indefinites beyond the matter of scope phenomena (but see Kripke 1977 and Ludlow and Neale 1991 for more extensive discussion), but will simply consider the question of whether Fodor and Sag's scope observations do in fact rule out a quantificational analysis.

Fodor and Sag note that in certain contexts (such as being embedded under propositional attitude verbs) specific indefinites seem to be able to take wider scope than is possible for other quantifiers:

(50) a. A man in Arizona thinks that every Gila monster in New Mexico emigrated to Canada.

    b. Every man in Arizona thinks that a Gila monster in New Mexico emigrated to Canada.

Whereas in (50b) the indefinite *a Gila monster in New Mexico* can take scope over the NP *every man in Arizona*, a universally quantified NP in the same position (as in (50a)) cannot take widest scope. One minor problematic aspect of this observation is that a full range of indefinites seem to share this property of being able to take wide scope (Ludlow and Neale 1991):[40]

(51) a. Every man in Arizona thinks that three Gila monsters in New Mexico sang at the Santa Fe Opera.

    b. Every man in Arizona thinks that several Gila monsters in New Mexico sang at the Santa Fe Opera.

    c. Every man in Arizona thinks that some Gila monsters in New Mexico sang at the Santa Fe Opera.

Additionally, although these facts are interesting, it is not clear that an explanation of them in and of itself necessarily rules out a quantificational analysis of indefinites.

What Fodor and Sag take as a more decisive argument against the quantificational analysis is an apparent limitation of scope possibilities for indefinites in sentences like the following:

(52) Each student overheard the rumor that a gila monster of mine drowned.

Fodor and Sag claim that the indefinite *a Gila monster of mine* can only take a narrowest scope and a widest scope reading, with the intermediate scope reading being impossible, as sketched out in (53).

(53) a. $\exists_x$ [x is a Gila monster] Every$_y$ [y is a student] y overheard the rumor that x drowned

    b. *Every$_y$ [y is a student] $\exists_x$ [x is a Gila monster] y overheard the rumor that x drowned

c. Every$_y$ [y is a student] y overheard the rumor that $\exists_x$ [x is a Gila monster] x drowned

Such a limitation would not be at all expected on a quantificational analysis. Fodor and Sag reason that if quantificational specific indefinites could somehow escape scope islands, then intermediate readings such as that represented in (53b) should also be possible. The full range of scope possibilities should be allowed. Since the intermediate reading is not available for (52), Fodor and Sag conclude that the apparent wide scope reading of the indefinite noted in (50) and (51) is actually a referential reading, rather than being quantificational in nature.

The problem here is that it is not at all clear that the absence of the reading in (53b) is due to the properties of the indefinite itself. There are in fact various strategies that can be applied to bring out the missing reading. One approach centers on the semantics of the head noun of the complex NP. As Ludlow and Neale (1991) point out, the noun *rumor* is problematic in that it may be difficult to discriminate individual instances of the same rumor, making scope interactions with distinct occurrences of a single rumor difficult to tease apart. As they demonstrate, if the noun is changed to *report*, intermediate scope or the indefinite becomes more apparent:

(54) Every student overheard three reports that a Gila monster of mine drowned.

Angelika Kratzer takes a different approach to bringing out the missing intermediate reading (see Rullmann 1989: fn. 7). She observes that the intermediate reading can be pragmatically forced in certain contexts. As an example she points out that the indefinite NP in the following sentence clearly can take intermediate scope:

(55) Each writer overheard the rumor that she didn't write a book she wrote.

Since there can be no self-contradicting rumors, *a book she wrote* must have scope outside of *the rumor* . . . , but it is at the same time within the scope of *each writer*. Thus, there are in fact "intermediate" readings of specific indefinites.

In summary, although the explanation of the scope properties of specific indefinites is by no means complete, the case against a quantificational analysis of specific indefinites is not completely persuasive. Additionally, the quantificational account I have developed has an advantage in that it permits an explanation of the various syntactic correlations with specificity noted in the preceding sections.

3.6 Conclusion

Investigating more closely the tree-splitting algorithm for mapping syntactic representations (assuming the VP-Internal Subject Hypothesis) to semantic representations from the point of view of the interpretation of indefinite NPs has led to the conclusion that there are actually two different kinds of indefinites, cardinal and presuppositional. Cardinal indefinites are essentially "existential closure indefinites" in that they receive their quantificational force from the operation of existential closure. Presuppositional indefinites form restrictive clause structures and therefore undergo the rule of QR.

In an extension of this initial proposal, I proposed that this distinction plays an essential role in characterizing the strong/weak distinction of Milsark (1974). In particular, I showed that the strong/weak contrast actually has a syntactic basis in that it results from the differential treatment of VP and IP in the derivation of logical representations from the intermediate syntactic level of LF. One consequence of this approach is that the presuppositional/nonpresuppositional contrast between strong and weak determiners noted by Milsark follows straightforwardly, as do the relative scope preference facts discussed by Ioup (1975).

This syntactic characterization of the strong/weak distinction in terms of presupposition also explains facts concerning antecedent-contained deletions. ACD requires that the object NP undergo QR (May 1985). Thus, ACD acts as a test for whether or not an NP must undergo QR, differentiating presuppositional and cardinal NPs—indefinites in ACD contexts must always receive the presuppositional interpretation.

Finally, I discussed the notion of "specificity" as it is used in a number of discussions of the interpretation of indefinites, and concluded that this idea of specificity corresponds quite directly to the concept of presuppositionality I had used to distinguish the two types of indefinites. In the next chapter I will take a closer look at the two possible interpretations for indefinites and show how they interact with extraction phenomena.

Chapter 4
Presupposition, Extraction, and Logical Form

4.1 Introduction

We have seen that indefinites can be either existential or presuppositional. I begin this chapter by further refining this classification of indefinites. The revised taxonomy will then prove useful in looking at further instances where the syntax and semantics of NPs interact. The initial syntactic phenomenon I focus on here is that of extraction from "picture" NPs of various types. I examine the varying acceptability of this type of extraction with verbs of various types, as well as NPs of different types. I show that it is actually the interpretation of the NP that is crucial in determining extractability, and that the choice of verb can influence the likelihood of a particular interpretation (either presuppositional or cardinal) being preferred. That is, certain verbs seem to preferentially select one or the other of the two readings. This way of characterizing the differences among different verbs is supported by data involving a number of different constructions that distinguish between presuppositional and cardinal NPs. Finally, these conclusions are given additional support by some very interesting parallel phenomena in German involving the semantic and syntactic effects of scrambling.

4.2 A Taxonomy of Indefinites

In chapter 3 I examined a number of contrasts between what I called cardinal and presuppositional indefinites. (This division should not be confused with the split into weak and strong NPs—weak NPs can be either cardinal or presuppositional, whereas strong NPs are only presuppositional.) These differences can be summarized as shown in (1).

(1) *Two types of indefinites*
   Cardinal   Presuppositional
   Do not undergo QR   Undergo QR
   Form cardinality predicates   Form operator-variable structures

In the simplest cases, the possibility of showing either the cardinal or the presuppositional reading depends on the choice of determiner in the NP. The strong determiners (e.g., *the*, *every*, *each*, *most*, and *all*) permit only the presuppositional reading. This reading arises from the fact that they undergo QR, by which they adjoin to IP . Being at the IP level of the syntactic tree, the strong NPs are then mapped into a restrictive clause by the tree-splitting procedure. Strong determiners have quantificational force; they function as operators binding the variable(s) introduced in the restrictive clause.

The weak determiners (*some*, *many*, *several, few*, as well as the numerals) are ambiguous between the cardinal and the presuppositional readings. On their presuppositional reading they undergo QR just as the strong NPs do. On their cardinal reading they remain within VP at LF and are mapped into the nuclear scope by the tree-splitting process. On the cardinal reading the weak indefinites are bound by existential closure (hence, I also call them existential closure indefinites). Thus, on the existential closure reading a weak determiner has no quantificational force; it functions as a cardinality predicate. Thus, the possibility of an NP having one or the other interpretation is determined (in part) by its syntax.

As it stands, the chart in (1) does not cover all indefinite NP types. For example, there is still the question of where generic indefinite NPs fit into the classification of indefinites (recall the discussion of the generic interpretation of bare plurals in chapter 2). Generics do not have quantificational force of their own, since there is no determiner functioning as an operator. Nonetheless, generic bare plurals show some of the semantic and syntactic properties of the presuppositional indefinites. They are introduced in a restrictive clause in the logical representation. On the syntactic side, generics also license antecedent-contained deletion (ACD), which is an indicator of a QR interpretation of an NP (the generic interpretation in this case is brought out by the adverb of quantification *usually*):

(2) a.   Oscar usually reads books that Olga does.
    b. *?Oscar read books that Olga did.

The generic sentence in (2a) permits ACD, but the episodic sentence in (2b) (which does not readily permit a generic interpretation for the indefinite owing to the absence of the adverb) does not. Thus, although generic indefinites do not have quantificational force of their own (they are bound by either the abstract generic operator *Gen* or an appropriate adverb of quantification), they do undergo QR and restrictive clause formation.

The classification of indefinites in (1) can be expanded to include the generics in a rather simple way. Given the range of interpretations discussed above, indefinites can be distinguished by two features representing their interpretive properties: [±quantificational force] (whether or not the NP has a determiner which functions as an operator) and [±QR] (whether or not the NP undergoes QR). Varying these two features yields three types of indefinites: generic, existential closure, and presuppositional (the fourth possible value, [+quantificational force, −QR], is of course contradictory). This yields the taxonomy shown in (3).

(3) *A taxonomy of indefinites*

	Generic	∃ Closure	Presuppositional
Q-force?	no	no	yes
QR?	yes	no	yes

Athough the feature characterization of the existential closure and presuppositional indefinites clearly follows from the analysis developed in chapter 3, the QR (restrictive clause) characterization of the quantificational reading of indefinite objects in *generic* contexts is not yet clearly motivated. Since I claimed that there is a close connection between the presuppositionality of an NP and the obligatoriness of QR, it is not immediately obvious where the notion of presuppositionality fits in the interpretation of generics. Put in another way, if the quantificational reading involves a restrictive clause, which in turn is associated with QR and presupposition, how do we end up with generic indefinites (which at first blush appear to not presuppose existence) in the restrictive clause?

To answer this question, we need to take a closer look at the semantics of generic indefinites. In a recent discussion of indefinites, Kratzer considers the problem of generic quantifier phrases such as those I have been referring to as undergoing QR.[1] The problem here is that although these NPs are associated with QR and restrictive clause formation, they do not seem to give rise to existential presuppositions, as observed by Strawson (1952):

(4) a. All trespassers on this land will be prosecuted.
    b. All moving bodies not acted upon by external forces continue in a
       state of uniform motion in a straight line.

The sentences in (4) are taken to express truths (rather than being false or
even undefined with respect to truth-value) even though there may not be
any trespassers or moving bodies existing at a given time.[2]

In unraveling this apparent conflict between genericity and presuppositionality, Kratzer suggests that generic sentences are all implicitly mod-
alized in the sense that an implicit modal (necessity) operator is prefixed
to the whole sentence. As in other modal constructions, the exact nature
of the necessity will differ according to the context. For example, (4a)
involves a "legal necessity," whereas (4b) involves necessity in view of the
laws of nature. (For a more complete discussion of modality, see Kratzer
1981.)

Like other operators (apart from the existential closure operator), modal
operators take some sort of a restrictor. Assuming that an NP such as *all
trespassers* in (4a) *does* give rise to a presupposition that there are trespassers, presupposition accommodation (as discussed in chapter 3) applies
to give the result that the presupposition induced by the quantifier phrase
is interpreted as a restriction for the modal operator, following Kratzer
(1981):

(5) [□: There are trespassers] [All trespassers will be prosecuted]

Kratzer gives the interpretation of (5) as follows: (5) is true in a world if
and only if in all those trespasser-containing worlds w' that come closest
to what the law provides in w, all trespassers will be prosecuted. Since the
presupposition is interpreted as a restriction for the modal operator, the
generic sentence itself (represented in the right-hand clause in (5)) does not
carry any existential commitment with respect to trespassers. As noted by
Kratzer, this analysis carries over to generic bare plurals as well. There are
in fact existence presuppositions in sentences with generic bare plurals, but
these presuppositions are accommodated into the restrictor of the implicit
modal.

Thus, the observations I made above concerning the three-way classification of indefinites are consistent with the approach to quantification I
developed in chapter 3 in the sense that the [+QR] feature can indeed be
associated with QR and restrictive clause formation to distinguish both
generic and "presuppositional" indefinites from the existential closure
indefinites (I continue to use the term *presuppositional* to distinguish NPs
with a "strong" interpretation from generics). In the rest of this chapter I

will utilize the three-way distinction among indefinites given in (3) to examine a number of syntactic phenomena in which the interpretation of an NP plays a crucial role.

4.3 Extraction from NP: Some Initial Observations

The problem of extraction from "picture" NPs has been much discussed in the literature. In particular, it has long been noted that there is a contrast between definite and indefinite NPs with respect to extraction (Chomsky 1973, 1977, Erteschik-Shir 1973, Fiengo and Higginbotham 1981, Bowers 1988):

(6) a. Who did you see a picture of?
    b. *Who did you see the picture of?

Fiengo and Higginbotham attribute the contrast in (6) to a Specificity Condition: Extraction from "specific" NPs is not possible, where specific NPs are those "having or purporting to have some definite reference" (1981:412). This is not a very precise characterization by any means, and although Fiengo and Higginbotham do remark that "quantifiers of some sorts produce specificity," in general their discussion and examples deal mainly with definite (in the limited sense in which the determiner = *the*) versus indefinite NPs (determiner = *a*). An obvious question is whether this use of "specificity" can be assimilated to the presuppositional characterization of specificity developed in chapter 3. An examination of different NP types shows that there is in fact a distinction between strong and weak NPs with respect to extraction:

(7) a.   Who did you see pictures of?
    b.   Who did you see a picture of?
    c.   Who did you see many pictures of?
    d.   Who did you see several pictures of?
    e.   Who did you see some pictures of?

(8) a. *?Who did you see the picture of?
    b. *?Who did you see every picture of?
    c. *?Who did you see most pictures of?
    d. *?Who did you see each picture of?
    e. ??Who did you see the pictures of?

The examples in (7) show that extraction from NPs with weak determiners such as *a*, *many*, and *some* is quite acceptable. This contrasts with the examples in (8), where extraction from NPs with strong determiners (*the*, *every*, *each*, ...) is shown to be bad.[3]

Looking more closely, we see that the contrast does not simply arise from the choice of determiner. If a presuppositional interpretation is induced by the determiner combination *a certain*, the acceptability of extraction is also reduced. Extraction from these NPs appears to be awkward in much the same way as extraction from clearly definite NPs, whereas extraction from a nonpresuppositional indefinite is fine:

(9) a. *Who did Mary say you saw a certain picture of?
    b. *Who did Mary say you saw the picture of?
    c.   Who did Mary say you saw a picture of?

Thus, the "specificity" effect is not due to a contrast between the definite and indefinite determiners, or even between strong and weak determiners. Although extraction from an NP with a strong determiner is generally bad, the acceptability of extraction from an NP with a weak determiner hinges on there being no presuppositional reading available (or required) in the given context.[4]

Thus, there clearly seems to be some kind of connection between the extraction facts I have presented in this section and the semantico-syntactic properties of NPs that I developed in the previous chapter. The issue that remains to be investigated is just what the nature of this connection is, and how it is to be represented in the grammar. How does the notion of presuppositionality interact with the purely syntactic operation of extraction to produce the contrasts noted above? There have been a number of attempts to explain the extraction-from-NP contrasts. Although none of them approaches the problem exactly on these terms, an examination of some of the various analyses is useful in that they each raise questions and problems (beyond those raised by Chomsky (1973) and Fiengo and Higginbotham (1981)) that must be considered in giving a more complete account. Therefore, in the following sections I will attempt to define the problem of extraction from NP more completely by bringing a fuller range of observations to bear on the issue.

4.3.1 A Purely Syntactic Explanation: Subjacency

Bowers (1988) gives an explanation of the "specificity effects" that draws upon work on the structure of the NP in English and other languages. Bowers's analysis is based on the idea that NPs with strong determiners and NPs with weak determiners differ in structural complexity, making use of the notion of a *determiner phrase* (DP).[5] In the *DP Hypothesis* the determiner (D) of an NP is taken to be a functional element analogous to

Infl at the sentence level, which thus heads the NP, rather than the noun itself functioning as the head (Abney 1987).

Bowers utilizes the DP/NP contrast to account for "specificity effects" by proposing that strong and weak NPs differ in structure. Following Jackendoff (1968, 1977), Bowers divides quantifiers into two groups: Class I (strong) and Class II (weak). He proposes that Class I quantifiers are of category D, whereas Class II quantifiers are adjectives and attach within NP:[6]

(10) a. [DP each [NP picture of manatees]]   STRONG

    b. [NP [AP many][N' pictures of manatees]]   WEAK.

Thus, the strong NPs differ from the weak NPs in that they have an additional layer of structure on top of their NP structure, as shown in (10a), whereas weak NPs consist of only NP, as shown in (10b).

This structural distinction between strong and weak NPs leads to an explanation of the extraction contrasts in terms of Subjacency. Extraction from a weak NP crosses only an NP boundary, whereas in the case of a strong NP the extracted *wh*-phrase crosses an NP *and* a DP boundary. Bowers assumes that in the case of extraction out of a weak NP object the NP is L-marked by the verb and thus is not a blocking category. In the case of extraction from a DP (an NP with a strong determiner), the NP is not L-marked by the verb, owing to the presence of the intervening maximal projection DP. Therefore, the NP is a blocking category, and a barrier, and the DP "inherits" barrierhood from the NP. This results in the extraction crossing two barriers, creating a Subjacency violation (Chomsky 1986a):

(11) a. who, did you see [NP[AP many] [N' pictures [PP of t,]]]

    b. who, did you see [DP the [NP[N' picture [PP of t,]]]

Regardless of whether his assumptions about L-marking and its effects in NPs versus DPs can be maintained, Bowers's account runs into problems because extraction-from-NP phenomena are a great deal more variable than would be expected under a pure subjacency approach. Since ill-formedness results from the structure of the NP, which is a reflection of the category of its determiner, an obvious problem for this account is the ambiguity of weak quantifiers. Weak quantifiers can have either a cardinal or a presuppositional reading. Within Bowers's explanation, this would mean that weak quantifiers would have to be capable of acting as either

adjectives (the cardinal reading) or determiners that head DPs (the presuppositional reading).[7] Although this is not altogether implausible, there are
still other difficulties resulting from the fact that the acceptability of extraction is dependent on the choice of determiner.[8] Although variability
with weak NPs might be expressed in terms of a categorial ambiguity
reflecting their semantic ambiguity, strong determiners should always pro-
hibit extraction, since they are not ambiguous and will always induce a DP
structure in an NP. This prediction is not borne out. As pointed out to
me by Roger Higgins, there is an indefinite use of the (usually definite)
determiner *this*. The fact that in this usage *this* functions like a weak
determiner is shown by its ability to appear in *there*-sentences:

(12) There's this cow that I see every morning.

The indefinite use of *this* also seems to be permitted in extraction contexts:

(13) There's this cow that Egbert is painting this wonderful picture of.

Thus, the presence of a strong determiner in and of itself does not suffice
to rule out extraction. The possibility of extraction from "picture" nouns
seems to depend more on the actual interpretation of the NP than on the
choice of determiner.

  An even more serious problem is the fact that the acceptability of
extraction also appears to depend to some extent on the choice of the *verb*
(Erteschik-Shir 1973, Horn 1974):

(14) a. Who did you see a picture of?
      b. *Who did you destroy a picture of?

(15) a. Who did you read a book about?
      b. *Who did you tear up a book about?
      c. ?Who did you copyedit a book about?

All of the examples in (14) and (15) involve extraction out of an indefinite
NP, and they should all be equally good, since the extraction should not
cross any barriers, analogous to (11a). Yet for many speakers extraction
with the verbs *destroy*, *tear up*, and *copyedit* is noticeably less good than
in the case of *see* or *read*. Thus, it is clear that an account of extraction
from NP will also have to take into account NP-external factors such as
the choice of verb.

4.3.2 The Semantics of Verbs and Extraction from NP

Both Horn (1974) and Erteschik-Shir (1973) examine the role that the
choice of verb plays in extraction from NP objects. Horn takes as his

starting point the position that extraction out of an NP is in general not allowed:

(16) *The NP Constraint*

No constituent which is dominated by NP can be moved from that NP by a transformational rule. (Horn 1974:20)

This is a rather strong constraint, and although it accounts for the ungrammaticality of the sentences in (8) and (9), it still leaves the obvious problem of accounting for those cases in which extraction is permitted, such as those in (7). To explain these cases, Horn argues that sentences with "picture" NP objects are potentially structurally ambiguous. Thus, in (17a) the PP *about manatees* can potentially attach in one of two places: either to the NP or to the VP.

(17) a. Oscar read a book about manatees.
   b. [$_{IP}$ Oscar [$_{VP}$ read [$_{NP}$ a book [$_{PP}$ about manatees]]]].
   c. [$_{IP}$ Oscar [$_{VP}$ read [$_{NP}$ a book] [$_{PP}$ about manatees]]].
   d. What did Oscar read a book about?

The bracketing in (17b) shows the PP attached to the NP, and the bracketing in (17c) shows the PP attached to the VP. In (18) and (19) I give tree representations of the two VPs.

(18) *PP-attached-to-NP*

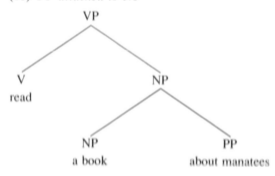

(19) *PP-attached-to-VP*

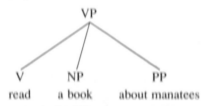

Most importantly, in (17c) the PP is *not* contained within the object NP. Thus, if the sentence in (17a) is indeed ambiguous between these two structures, the fact that extraction of the PP is possible (as shown in (17d)) does not constitute a counterexample to the NP Constraint; the extraction structure is simply derived from the structure in (19). Extraction of a PP attached to VP does not violate the NP Constraint.

Horn claims that verbs like *destroy* permit only one structure (presumably by the subcategorization frames): the structure in which the PP attaches to NP, shown in (18). Thus, *destroy* does not permit extraction from NP (as shown in (14)) because it does not subcategorize for the structure that makes the extraction possible.[9]

A major problem with Horn's analysis (beyond those discussed in note 9) is that it focuses entirely on the differences between verbs. As we have already seen, the constraints on extraction involve properties of the NP itself as well. Horn's account does not explain why even in the case of verbs like *read* and *write* the extraction is more acceptable with NPs with weak determiners than with NPs with strong determiners. Another question is the *source* of the differences between verbs—why should verbs like *destroy* permit only the structure in (18)? The fact that there are particular semantic classes of verbs and NPs involved in the extraction contrasts is still left unexplained.

Erteschik-Shir (1973) approaches this problem from the point of view that the presence or absence of what she calls "semantic dominance" in the extraction domain leads to contrasts in extractability. Thus, the extractability contrasts between strong and weak NPs (repeated in (20) and (21)) are explained by the fact that strong NPs in general must be semantically dominant, whereas weak NPs need not be.

(20) a. *?Who did you see the picture of?
     b. *Who did you write every book about?
     c. *What did you paint most pictures of?
     d. *Who did you read all books by?

(21) a. Who did you see a picture of?
     b. Who did you write some books about?
     c. What did you paint many pictures of?
     d. Who did you read several books by?

Erteschik-Shir defines semantic dominance in terms of whether or not a contextual reference is present. Thus, these observations appear to be related (theoretically as well as empirically) to the observations made in chapter 3 concerning presuppositionality in NPs. As an initial attempt to recast Erteschik-Shir's observations within the framework developed here, the contrasts between (20) and (21) can be described by the following constraint on extraction from presuppositional NPs:

(22) *Presuppositional NP Constraint*
   Extraction cannot take place out of a presuppositional NP.

Erteschik-Shir also notes variation in extractability with different verbs, and it is interesting to see whether the presuppositionality approach can be extended to these cases as well (repeated from (14)–(15)):[10]

(23) a.   Who did you see a picture of?
   b.   *Who did you destroy a picture of?

(24) a.   Who did you read a book about?
   b.   *Who did you tear up a book about?
   c.   ?Who did you copyedit a book about?

The basic intuition here (to be discussed more thoroughly in a later section) is that "semantic dominance" arises in these cases because although destroying an object presupposes that the object exists (since the object is itself affected by the action), seeing and reading do not induce such a presupposition.

Erteschik-Shir relates a number of factors that influence the acceptability of extraction out of an NP to the notion of "semantic dominance." In some cases (such as the contrasts between strong and weak NPs) the relationship between her proposals concerning "dominance" and the differences between presuppositional and cardinal NPs that I discussed in the previous chapter is quite clear. In other cases (particularly involving contrasts between different verbs) the connection is less obvious.

In the next section I will examine the various extraction-from-NP contrasts in light of the ambiguity of indefinites. Tests that pick out the quantifier-raising interpretation of an NP will be useful in pinning down how the choice of verb can affect the presuppositionality of its NP object. This in turn will bring us closer to the ultimate goal of going beyond a simple descriptive generalization concerning the effects of "semantic dominance" (or presupposition) and replacing it with a more explanatory account deriving the extraction constraint in (22) from more general principles in the grammar.

4.4   Quantification and Extraction from NP

In examining several previous approaches to the problem of extractions
from NP, I have adduced three additional "complicating factors" (beyond
the initial observations) that affect the acceptability of such extractions.
These are (1) the determiner of the NP (strong NPs are less amenable to
extraction than weak NPs), (2) the type of verb governing the NP (verbs
like *read* and *write* permit extraction, whereas with verbs like *destroy*
extraction is less acceptable), and (3) the role of (some notion of) presupposition. This raises a number of questions. First, why should two such
apparently unrelated factors as (1) and (2) both result in reduced grammaticality in extraction contexts? Ideally, there should be some common
ground between the two that explains why the NP determiners and the
verb types should have this effect. Second, where does presupposition fit
in, and how can such a semantic notion be related to a syntactic phenomenon like an extraction contrast? And finally, the extraction contrasts are
"fragile" in the sense of being vague and likely to vanish in certain contexts. An analysis of the extraction phenomena should also account for
this vagueness.

As a starting point, I examine the varying acceptability of extraction
from NP in light of the results in chapter 3 concerning the interpretation
of NPs. I show that the particular semantic properties of the different
predicate types can be characterized in terms of the interpretation(s) of
object NPs that they favor. Pursuing Erteschik-Shir's initial suggestions
concerning the role of "semantic dominance" in extraction contexts, I try
to explain the contrasts noted above by showing that certain transitive
verbs require some sort of preexistence of their objects in the form of a
presuppositional reading involving QRing of the object. This preexistence
in turn results in a quantificational environment that rules out cardinal
NPs, and therefore rules out extraction. Extraction is ruled out in these
cases because extraction is only possible from an NP that is not required to
undergo QR. This in turn leads to an account of the vagueness of the
judgments involved. It is not surprising that the interpretation of an NP
should vary with context, and to the extent that extractability is dependent
on a particular interpretation the judgments concerning extraction should
vary as well.

4.4.1   An Ambiguity with Indefinite Objects

Adverbs of quantification like *always* can serve as a useful tool in high-
lighting the quantificational variability of indefinites. In the context of an

adverb of quantification an indefinite NP in object position can receive two possible readings, depending on whether or not it receives its quantificational force from the adverb. I will refer to the first of these readings as *quantificational* or *presuppositional*, by which I mean that it involves raising of the indefinite object by QR so that it forms a restrictive clause. The object behaves like a variable, and is bound by the adverb of quantification. The second type of reading is purely existential; again the object NP has no quantificational force of its own, but it is in this case bound by existential closure. Following the lines of the discussion in chapter 3, I will call this the *existential* or the *existential closure* reading of the indefinite. ,

These two readings are most readily brought out in generic, or habitual contexts (such as those containing adverbs of quantification like *usually* and *always* in conjunction with the present tense). The contrast between these two types of readings is shown in (25), where I have given contexts that highlight each of the two readings:

(25) a. I always write up a witty story about Millard Fillmore.
    b. Quantificational reading: Whenever I hear a witty story about Millard Fillmore, I always write it up.
    c. Existential reading: First thing in the morning, I always write up a witty story about Millard Fillmore.

The quantificational reading involves the binding of a variable corresponding to *a witty story about Millard Fillmore* by the adverb of quantification *always*. Following Lewis (1975), I assume that the representation of the quantificational reading given in (25b) is as follows:

(26) Always$_x$ [x is a story about Millard Fillmore] I write up x

As shown in (26), the indefinite object NP is introduced in the restrictive clause. Given the account of quantification I presented earlier, restrictive clause formation is associated with raising of an NP by QR to adjoin to IP; where the tree-splitting algorithm ensures that it will be mapped into a restrictive clause. Thus, the quantificational reading in (25b) is associated with the application of QR to the object NP.

The existential reading requires some (perhaps implicit) context variable for the adverb of quantification to bind. In (25c) I have given a context in which *always* quantifies over "morning situations," resulting in the logical representation shown in (27).

(27) Always$_t$ [t is in the morning] $\exists_x$ x is a story about Millard Fillmore $\land$ I write up x at t

Thus, in (27) the variable introduced by the NP *a witty story about Millard Fillmore* is not bound by *always*; it is bound instead by existential closure. The NP is *not* raised by QR, since it is not incorporated into the restrictive clause.

The two readings of indefinite objects that I have presented here will prove to be important in answering the questions concerning extraction from NP that I posed earlier. Though the contrast is subtle, it can be highlighted by the choice of contexts, as I have shown. There are also a number of syntactic constructions that are sensitive to the distinction between the two readings of the indefinites. In the following subsections I will present these additional contexts that can serve as tests for clearly distinguishing the two readings.

4.4.2 Antecedent-Contained Deletions and Ambiguity

One context in which the difference between the existential and the quantificational readings is brought out is that of ACD, which I discussed in the previous chapter. As I noted, ACD is possible only in those contexts where QR has taken place. Given the relationship between QR and the "quantificational," or presuppositional reading of the indefinite posited above, it is expected that ACD should rule out the existential closure (non-QR) reading for an indefinite object in generic contexts. This does in fact seem to be the case:

(28) a. I usually read books that you do.
     b. Quantificational reading: Whenever you read (some) books,
         I usually read them too.
     c. *Existential reading: Usually (in the morning) I read books that
         you read too.

in (28) the ACD with an indefinite object is made possible by the presence of the adverb *usually*, which induces a habitual reading for the sentence. The context of ACD, however, permits only one of the two logically possible interpretations for the indefinite object, as shown by the contexts given in (28b) and (28c). The existential reading corresponding to (28c) is ruled out.

4.4.3 *Any* and Ambiguity

Another context that distinguishes two readings for an object NP involves the use of the determiner *any*. The appearance of non-negative-polarity *any* as a determiner on an NP rules out the existential reading. An *any*-NP must have a quantificational reading, as shown in (29).

(29) I usually write up any story about Millard Fillmore.

This sentence can only have the quantificational reading; the existential reading is not possible. Thus, *any* provides another diagnostic for the quantificational reading.

As expected, the use of *any* is quite grammatical in ACD constructions. This fact also supports the correlation of *any* with the quantificational reading of an NP:

(30) I usually read any book you do.

These facts about any of course do not shed any light on the question of the nature of indefinites that I am considering here, but as a diagnostic for the availability of the quantificational reading they prove useful in investigating the distribution of the two readings with respect to various predicates.

4.4.4 German Scrambling and Indefinite Objects

German provides what may be the most "graphic" diagnostic for the QR reading of indefinite objects in generic contexts. German has a scrambling rule that allows constituents to move out of VP and adjoin to IP.[11] The VP-external position of the scrambled constituent is indicated by its position relative to a sentential adverb, which marks the VP boundary. Constituents to the left of the adverb are VP-external, constituents to the right of the adverb are generally interpreted as VP-internal.[12] (The literature on German scrambling is quite extensive. See Lenerz 1977, Lötscher 1983, Fanselow 1986, 1988b, Kathol 1989, Webelhuth 1989, and Moltmann 1991 for additional discussion.)

In the case of indefinite objects in generic contexts parallel to the English cases discussed above, the scrambled and unscrambled orders are distinguished semantically. In the case of the VP-internal or unscrambled order, the most neutral interpretation of the indefinite object is the existential closure interpretation.

(31) a. ... daß Otto immer Bücher über   Wombats liest.
        that Otto always books about wombats reads
     '... that Otto always reads books about wombats.'
  b. [$_{CP}$ daß [$_{IP}$ Otto immer [$_{VP}$ Bücher über Wombats liest]]]
  c. Always$_t$ [t is a time] $\exists_x$ x is a book $\wedge$ Otto reads x at t

The sentence in (31) shows the indefinite object in its base, or unscrambled, position. The interpretation for the sentence is given in (31c). The object

NP appears as a variable introduced in the nuclear scope, and is bound by existential closure.

This contrasts with the scrambled order. When the indefinite object is scrambled, the existential closure reading is no longer available, and the QR reading of the indefinite surfaces. The scrambled order is shown in (32).

(32) a. ... daß Otto Bücher über   Wombats immer liest.
           that Otto books   about wombats always reads
     b. [$_{CP}$ daß [$_{IP}$ Otto Bücher über Wombats immer [$_{VP}$ liest]]]
     c. Always$_x$ [x is a book] Otto reads x

The interpretation for the indefinite object in the sentence in (32) is the QR reading shown in (32c). Here the indefinite object is introduced in the restrictive clause, and is bound by the adverb of quantification *immer* 'always'.[13]

This contrast between scrambled and unscrambled orders with respect to the interpretation of the indefinite object can be explained by the Mapping Hypothesis if, as argued in Chapters 2 and 3, tree splitting can occur at S-structure in German. Thus, scrambling in German has the semantic effect of a sort of "S-structure QR" in sentences like (32).

Before leaping to the conclusion that S-structure scrambling in German is in fact *equivalent* to LF QR in English, a few observations are in order. First, it is not the case that scrambling acts as a total replacement for QR in German. If this were the case, we would expect that there would be no instances of scope ambiguity in German, and also that NPs that obligatorily undergo QR (namely, presuppositional NPs) would not be able to remain within VP at S-structure.[14] Neither of these predictions is borne out. Unscrambled sentences can show ambiguities of interpretation, and strong NPs may remain within VP at S-structure. In other words, S-structure scrambling need not occur, unlike QR, which presumably is required for quantificational NPs by some sort of condition on variable binding (see May 1977). Scrambling does have the effect of forcing the QR reading for a scrambled indefinite NP—scrambled NPs do not undergo LF lowering, and unscrambled indefinites usually do not receive the QR reading. In this sense, the effect of German S-structure scrambling is similar to the effect of the (morphological) accusative case marking in Turkish discussed in chapter 3.[15]

To summarize the preceding sections, an indefinite object NP has two potential readings in a generic context. The first is a quantificational reading that arises from the raising of the NP by QR to adjoin to IP, where it subsequently forms a restrictive clause in the semantic representation. The second reading is existential. In this case the NP is not raised by QR, but remains within the VP, and in the semantic representation it receives its existential force from the operation of existential closure. ACD once again serves as a diagnostic for the quantificational reading, since ACD is permitted only in contexts where the object NP must undergo QR. German scrambling contexts also serve to highlight the syntactic nature of the contrast between the two interpretations.

The next step is to investigate the connection between these two possible readings of indefinite objects and the various types of verbs discussed by Erteschik-Shir (1973) and Horn (1974). In the sections that follow I show that the type of verb determines which reading(s) of indefinite objects will be readily available. Additionally, I present data showing that the acceptability of German scrambling is also determined (in part) by the choice of predicate. Thus, the choice of verb determines whether or not quantifier raising of an indefinite object will be obligatory.

4.4.5 Verb Types and the Interpretation of Indefinites

Recall that both Erteschik-Shir (1973) and Horn (1974) observed that verbs differ in the extent to which they permit extraction from object NPs. In this section I examine three classes of verbs—the verbs of creation (such as *write* or *paint*), the verbs of "using" (such as *read* or *play*), and the "experiencer" verbs (such as *love* or *hate*)—in light of the discussion of indefinite interpretations above.

4.4.5.1 Creation versus Using: *Write/Read* The verbs of creation (*write, paint*, etc.) and the verbs of using (*read, play*, etc.) form two classes with respect to the behavior of "picture" noun objects. In particular, in this section I show that these two classes of verbs differ in the semantic interpretations they most readily permit for an indefinite object. The habitual contexts created by adverbs of quantification will serve as a diagnostic starting point for the discussion.

Considering first the verbs of using, the examples given in (33) (in generic contexts) all seem to permit both of the possible interpretations (quantificational and existential) for an indefinite "picture" noun object.

(33) a. I usually read a book by Robertson Davies.
   b. I usually play a sonata by Dittersdorf.
   c. I usually buy a picture of the Chiricahuas.
   d. I usually comment on an essay by George Will,
   e. I usually publish a book on Gila monsters.

All of the sentences in (33) are ambiguous (although in some cases one reading may be preferred over the other).

The availability of the quantificational reading can be further verified through the use of the tests presented in the preceding sections. For example, these verbs also permit *any*-NPs (which are an indicator of the quantificational reading) as their objects:

(34) a. I usually read any book by Robertson Davies.
    b. I usually play any sonata by Dittersdorf.
    c. I usually buy any picture of the Chiricahuas.
    d. I usually comment on any essay by George Will.
    e. I usually publish any book on Gila monsters.

Another indicator of a QR reading is ACD. In the generic context produced by the adverb *usually* ACD is also possible with the verbs of using:

(35) a. I usually read books that you do.
    b. Evelina usually buys pictures that Egbert does.

 Of course, in the sentences in (35) the object NP receives only the quantificational (QR) reading.

The final correlation with the quantificational reading I gave above involved German scrambling. In the case of German verbs of using, scrambling is permitted (as indicated by the position of the object to the left of the adverb) and yields the quantificational reading for the indefinite object:

(36) a. ... daß Otto Bücher über   Wombats immer liest.
          that Otto books   about wombats always reads
    b. $[_{CP}$ daß $[_{IP}$ Otto Bücher über Wombats immer $[_{VP}$ liest]]]
    c. Always$_x$ [x is a book] Otto reads x

Before proceeding further, it is important to note that one property common to all the verbs in the examples given in (33) is that they all can carry a possible implication that there be some preexisting books, sonatas, pictures, and essays. This is a crucial property of the quantificational reading. This property can be seen in paraphrases such as 'Whenever I encounter a sonata by Dittersdorf, I play it'. The *whenever*-clause in the paraphrase makes the notion of preexistence explicit. This notion of preexistence (as an existence presupposition) is also explicitly represented in the logical representation by the restrictive clause.

I now turn to the verbs of creating. These verbs denote the bringing of their objects into existence and therefore are incompatible with the notion of preexistence. Not surprisingly, these verbs do not permit a quantificational reading of an indefinite object:

(37) a. I usually write a book about slugs.
    b. I usually paint a picture of Barbary apes.
    c. I usually draw a map of Belchertown.

The sentences in (37) do not permit interpretations such as 'Whenever there is a book about slugs, I write it' or 'Whenever there is a map of Belchertown, I draw it'. Thus, one might say that things that are only just brought into existence cannot be mapped into a restrictive clause, and are limited to only the cardinal (existential) reading. *Any*-NPs are also quite strange in these contexts:

(38) a. *I usually write any book about slugs.
    b. *I usually paint any picture of Barbary apes.
    c. *I usually draw any map of Belchertown.

The absence of the quantificational reading also correlates with the inability of the verbs of creating to appear in ACD contexts. ACD requires the quantificational interpretation and is therefore expected to be unacceptable with verbs of creation like *write* and *paint*. This prediction also seems to be borne out:

(39) a. *I usually write answers that you do.
    b. *I usually draw animals that you do.
    c. *I usually paint designs that you do.

I have deliberately chosen sentences that do not pragmatically rule out ACD in that they permit repetition of the action involved.[16] Though it might be hard to imagine two people writing the same books, it is perfectly plausible that two people should write the same answers on a test. Thus, the sentences in (39) provide additional support for the idea that the quantificational reading is not readily available for some verbs.

Finally, in German the verbs of creation do not allow scrambling of an indefinite object in normal contexts (but see Kathol 1989 for discussion of some unusual uses of creation verbs). As shown in (40), the unscrambled order (with the object NP to the right of the sentential adverb *immer* 'always') is perfectly acceptable, but this ordering permits only the existential closure interpretation of the object.

(40) a. ... daß Otto immer Bücher über   Wombats schreibt.
        that Otto always books about wombats writes
        '... that Otto always writes books about wombats (e.g., in the
        summer when he has finished all his term papers).'
      b. Always$_t$ [t is a time] $\exists_x$ x is a book $\wedge$ Otto writes x at t

(41) *... daß Otto Bücher über Wombats immer schreibt.

In contrast to the unscrambled order, the scrambled order given in (41) is
ungrammatical.

Thus, the interpretations of habitual sentences with adverbs of quantification show that the verbs of using and creation differ strikingly in the
readings they permit for an indefinite object. The verbs of using allow both
the quantificational reading and the existential closure reading, whereas
the verbs of creation permit only the existential closure reading. This
observation is supported by three tests that act as indicators for the QR
reading of an NP: the acceptability of the determiner *any*, ACD, and
scrambling of indefinites in German. In the next section I look at the
experiencer predicates, which show yet another pattern of effects.

4.4.5.2 The Quantificational Reading and Experiencer Verbs   In the previous section I showed that there is a class of verbs, those of creation, that
do not permit a quantificational reading for an indefinite object. Just as
there are verbs that seem to be limited to the existential reading of the
object, there are also predicates that permit only a quantificational reading
of an indefinite object NP in the context of an adverb of quantification.
These cases are those in which there is no possibility of the adverb of
quantification binding some sort of contextual variable as in (27). One
particular case involves the experiencer verbs. Experiencer verbs constitute
a special case of the so-called individual-level predicates discussed in chapter 2 (the predicates roughly corresponding to permanent states). Before
discussing experiencer predicates in detail, I will briefly review some of the
relevant properties of individual-level predicates.

As I discussed in chapter 2, Kratzer (1989) argues that stage-level
(denoting temporary states) and individual-level (permanent state) predicates differ with respect to variable binding. Stage-level predicates have an
abstract spatiotemporal argument that can act as a variable in quantificational contexts. Individual-level predicates, on the other hand, do not
have this spatiotemporal argument (I follow Kratzer's notation here):

(42) a. When Betty speaks Hittite, she speaks it well.
      b. Always$_l$ [speaks (Betty, Hittite, l)] speaks-well (Betty, Hittite, l)

(43) a. *When Betty knows Hittite, she knows it well.

   b. *Always [knows (Betty, Hittite)] knows-well (Betty, Hittite)

(42) and (43) illustrate the contrast between the two types of predicates. In the case of the stage-level predicate *speaks*, the adverb of quantification *always* (implicit in the *when*-clause, according to Lewis (1975) and Kratzer (1986)) binds the spatiotemporal variable l, and the resulting logical representation is well formed. In the case of the individual-level predicate *know*, this variable is not available, and the logical representation yields a vacuous quantification, since there are no other possible variables in (43a) for the quantificational adverb to bind. Assuming that there is a general prohibition on vacuous quantification in natural language (along the lines of that proposed by Milsark (1974), for example), the ungrammaticality of (43a) is thereby accounted for.

Returning to the question of the interpretation of indefinites, there is a clear prediction to be tested. If a situation existed in which there was an adverb of quantification and an indefinite object NP was the only potential variable for the operator (such as *always*) to bind, we would expect that only the quantificational reading of the indefinite would be possible. To show just how this sort of situation can come about, it is useful to exploit the variable-binding differences between stage- and individual-level predicates.

Since stage-level predicates can always bind an abstract spatiotemporal variable, we would not expect the quantificational interpretation of an indefinite object to be required in these cases. This is in fact what is seen in (33) and (37): the quantificational interpretation is certainly not required, and in some cases (such as (37)) it is not even possible. Individual-level predicates, on the other hand, do not have the option of binding a spatiotemporal variable. Thus, it should be possible to construct examples in which an indefinite object NP *must* receive a quantificational interpretation. In (44) I give some examples of sentences containing an experiencer predicate, which functions as an individual-level predicate, along with an adverb of quantification (*usually, generally*).[17] In addition, since the subject is the pronoun *I*, the only variable for the adverb to bind is the indefinite object NP.

(44) a. I usually like a picture of manatees.

   b. I usually love a sonata by Dittersdorf.

   c. I usually appreciate a good joke about violists.

   d. I generally hate an article about carpenter ants.

   e. I generally detest an opera by Wagner.

    f. I usually dislike a movie about vampires.

    g. I generally abhor a book about Brussels sprouts.

    h. I usually despise a painting of Chester A. Arthur.

    i. I generally loathe a story about stockbrokers.

The sentences in (44) only permit the quantificational interpretation for the object NP. Thus, (44a) can only mean 'Whenever I see a picture of manatees, I like it'. It cannot mean something like 'Every morning I treat myself to liking a picture of manatees', which would be an existential reading for the object NP. Likewise, (44e) can only mean 'Whenever I hear an opera by Wagner, I detest it'. An existential reading such as 'When I need to express anger, I detest an opera by Wagner' is not possible. Casting this observation in terms of the discussion of the difference between the existential reading and the quantificational reading with respect to quantifier raising and logical representations, we have the result that the sentences in (44) all require that the object NP be raised by QR in the mapping to the logical representation.

    If, as I have suggested, the quantificational reading is strongly preferred for indefinite objects of experiencer verbs in generic contexts, then it should also be the case that ACD should be possible in these environments:

(45) a. I usually like pictures that you do.

      b. I usually love animals that you do.

      c. I generally appreciate jokes that you do.

      d. ?I usually hate articles that you do.

      e. I generally detest operas that you do.

      f. I usually dislike movies that you do.

      g. ?I generally abhor books that you do.

      h. I generally despise paintings that you do.

      i. ?I generally loathe stories that you do.

Although there is some variation in acceptability in the sentences in (45), they are all clearly more acceptable than those in (39), which involve verbs of creation for which the quantificational reading of the indefinite object is not permitted.

    Another indicator that objects of experiencer verbs readily receive a quantificational interpretation is the fact that *any*-NPs are also quite acceptable as objects to these verbs:

(46) a. I usually like any book about scorpions.

      b. I usually love any opera by Mozart.

   c. I usually detest any meal with Brussels sprouts.

   d. I usually hate any movie about vampires.

Thus, the various tests for the QR reading in English show that it is quite clear that experiencer verbs permit the QR reading of an indefinite.

Finally, in German the experiencer verbs are remarkable in that they not only permit scrambling, but also seem to prefer it. This is significant, since the scrambled order permits only the quantificational reading of an indefinite object:

(47) a. .. daß Otto Bücher über Wombats immer mag.

         that Otto books about wombats always likes

        '... that Otto always likes books about wombats.'

     b. Always$_x$ [x is a book] Otto likes x

(48) a. ... weil Olga Opern von Mozart immer schätzt.

         since Olga operas by Mozart always appreciates

        '... since Olga always appreciates operas by Mozart.'

     b. Always$_x$ [x is an opera] Olga appreciates x

In summary, the experiencer verbs appear to have the property that they "select" the quantificational (QR) reading of an indefinite object in generic contexts. This peculiarity is explained within the analysis of stage- and individual-level predicates of Kratzer (1989) by the absence of a spatio-temporal argument in the case of experiencer predicates, which fall into the individual-level class. The observations about the available reading are corroborated by the ACD data in English and the scrambling facts in German. In the next section I return to the question of extraction from NP, showing how it interacts with the possible interpretations of indefinite NP objects and thereby also with the verb type involved in the sentence.

4.4.6 English: Extraction and Ambiguity

Having presented the two possible readings for an indefinite object and also their distribution with respect to various verb types, I now investigate the interaction of extraction from "picture" NPs with the potential interpretations of the object NP in (25a). In particular, I show not only that extraction rules out the quantificational reading of an indefinite object, but also that extractability (i.e., the grammaticality of extraction) is correlated with the availability of the existential closure interpretation of the object NP. In other words, extraction is only possible when the existential reading is possible. The differences among the various verbs with respect to extraction thus mirror the differences with respect to which interpretations are favored for indefinite objects with particular verbs.

The first step is to consider the effect extraction has on the available readings for an indefinite object in the case of verbs that allow both interpretations. Although indefinite object NPs with verbs of using like *read, play,* and *tell* are ambiguous (in generic contexts) between the existential (cardinal) and quantificational interpretations, when extraction out of a "picture" NP object occurs, it has the effect of eliminating the possibility of the quantificational reading:

(49) a. What do you usually read books about?
     b. Who do you usually play sonatas by?
     c. What do you usually tell jokes about?

The extractions in (49) are grammatical, but only in a context that permits an existential interpretation. On the reading corresponding to the quantificational reading the extraction is considerably less felicitous.

Given the relationship between the "quantificational" reading and QR that I discussed above, the elimination of the quantificational reading by extraction suggests that extractability is related to nonpresuppositionality in the object NP. This, in turn, suggests that Erteschik-Shir's (1973) approach to extraction from NP is on the right track. In other words, extraction seems to be prohibited from quantificational, or presuppositional, NPs. Before considering why this constraint might exist, I further pursue the parallel to Erteschik-Shir's observations by examining the possible interpretations with various verb types.

First I consider the differences between verbs of using and verbs of creation. As I noted above, extraction is possible from objects of verbs of using. When extraction occurs, only the existential reading of the object is permitted, regardless of the preference shown by the verb:

(50) a. Who do you usually read a book by?
     b. Who do you usually play a sonata by?
     c. What do you usually buy a picture of?
     d. Who do you usually comment on an essay by?
     e. What do you usually publish a book about?

Creation predicates allow only the existential reading for an indefinite object. As might be expected, extraction is possible from these predicates:

(51) a. What do you usually write a book about?
     b. What do you usually paint a picture of?
     c. Which town do you usually draw a map of?

Thus, although the verbs *read* and *write* differ in whether or not they permit the presuppositional reading for an indefinite NP object, both verbs easily permit extraction from a "picture" NP object. This shows that the correlation between the availability of the existential interpretation and the possibility of extraction holds at least in one direction. When the existential reading is possible, extraction is also possible.

Turning again to the experiencer predicates, we can test this correlation in the other direction. If the hypothesis that extraction is possible only when the NP need *not* be raised by QR is correct, then extraction should be ruled out (even for indefinites) when a quantificational interpretation is obligatory. In other words, extraction should be ruled out where the existential reading is not available. This hypothesis can be tested by considering "picture" NP objects of experiencer verbs, since the experiencer verbs are a case where quantifier raising of an indefinite object appears to be required. Because of the absence of the spatiotemporal variable, it is easy to construct contexts where only the quantificational reading is possible using these verbs:

(52) a. Egbert usually loves sonatas by Dittersdorf.
   b. Olga usually likes paintings of Brussels sprouts.
   c. Evelina usually despises books by Augustus F. Whipple.
   d. Oscar usually hates jokes about violists.

The following examples show that extraction from objects of experiencer verbs is in fact at best awkward:[18]

(53) a. *What do you usually like a picture of?
   b. *Who do you usually love a sonata by?
   c. *What do you usually appreciate a good joke about?
   d. *What do you usually hate an article about?
   e. *Who do you generally detest an opera by?
   f. *What do you usually dislike a movie about?
   g. *What do you generally abhor a book about?
   h. *Who do you generally despise a painting of?
   i. *Who/What do you generally loathe a story about?

In summary, the experiencer verb data show that when the existential reading of an indefinite object NP is ruled out (as it is with these verbs), extraction from the NP is ruled out as well. Thus, it appears that there is indeed a correlation between extractability and the availability of the existential reading. Extraction is possible if (and only if) the existential (non-QR) reading is available. This conclusion supports the informal account of extraction in terms of presuppositionality that I proposed above. In the next section I look again at German and show that there is also a correlation between extraction from NPs and word order.

4.4.7 German: Extraction and Scrambling

In the previous section I showed that there is a connection between extraction from NP and the existential closure reading in English. In this section I examine the parallel case in German. Although German does not allow extraction from "picture" nouns in the same way that English does, there are other cases of extraction out of an NP in German. One of these is the *was-für* split, which I discussed in chapter 2. In the *was-für* split the *was* portion of the NP specifier *was-für* 'what kind of' breaks off and is fronted to [Spec, CP], leaving the rest of the NP behind:

(54) Was$_i$ hast du t$_i$ für Bücher gelesen?
$\llcorner$————————$\lrcorner$

what have you for books read
'What kind of books have you read?'

In this section I show that the *was-für* split in German is constrained in much the same way as the English extraction from "picture" noun objects. Extraction is only possible from indefinite objects that can have the existential closure interpretation. What makes the German case interesting is that the interpretation of the indefinite is to some extent determined by its *S-structure* position, as we saw in section 4.4.4. This makes the relationship between extraction and interpretation particularly salient, since scrambled indefinites (which have been moved out of VP) cannot have the existential closure interpretation.

If the correlation between extractability and the existential reading is in fact the correct generalization, there are certain predictions to be tested with respect to scrambling and extraction. In particular, extraction should only be possible from unscrambled indefinites. Scrambling of an indefinite object should rule out extraction. Looking first at verbs of using and creation, we see that this is in fact the case:[19]

(55) a. ... daß Otto immer Bücher über Wombats schreibt.
    that Otto always books about wombats writes
    '... that Otto is always writing books about wombats.'

   b. Was$_i$ hat Otto immer [$_{NP}$ t$_i$ für Bücher] geschrieben?
    what has Otto always   for books   written
    'What kind of books has Otto always written?'

(56) a. *... daß Otto Bücher über Wombats immer schreibt.
        that Otto books about wombats always writes
    b. *Was$_i$ hat Otto [$_{NP}$ t$_i$ für Bücher] immer geschrieben?
        what has Otto   for books   always written

With verbs of creation, only the unscrambled order (which gives the existential closure interpretation) is possible, and (not surprisingly) extraction from the NP is only possible in the unscrambled order as well. This can be seen in the contrast between the sentences in (55) and those in (56).

The fact that extraction is ruled out in the scrambled order in (56) is not unexpected regardless of whether or not there is a correlation between extraction and interpretation, since the scrambled "source" is also ungrammatical. To test whether or not there is a correlation between word order and extraction, we need to look at a case that allows both orders. Turning to the verbs of using, which do allow the scrambled order, we see that there is indeed a correlation between extraction and the unscrambled order.

(57) a. ... daß Hilda immer Sonaten von Dittersdorf spielt.
        that Hilda always sonatas by Dittersdorf plays
        '... that Hilda is always playing sonatas by Dittersdorf.'
    b. Was$_i$ hat Hilda immer [$_{NP}$ t$_i$ für Sonaten] gespielt?
        what has Hilda always   for sonatas   played
        'What kind of sonatas did Hilda always play?'
(58) a. ... daß Hilda Sonaten von Dittersdorf immer spielt.
        that Hilda sonatas by Dttersdorf always plays
        'If it is a sonata by Dittersdorf, Hilda plays it.'
    b. *Was$_i$ hat Hilda [$_{NP}$ t$_i$ für Sonaten] immer gespielt?
        what has Hilda   for sonatas   always played

In (57a) we see the unscrambled order, which yields the existential interpretation of the indefinite object. In (57b) we see that the *was-für* split is grammatical when the object is VP-internal (as indicated by its position to the right of the adverb). (58a) shows the scrambled order, in which the indefinite receives the quantificational interpretation, as indicated by the English translation,. In this case extraction is not possible, as shown by (58b). Thus, the verbs of using like *spielen* 'play' do permit extraction from NP, but only from an unscrambled (VP-internal) NP.[20]

Finally, I turn to the experiencer verbs. With the experiencer verbs, which require a quantificational interpretation, the unscrambled order is awkward, and the extraction from NP is correspondingly awkward, if not ungrammatical:[21]

(59) a. ??... daß Olga immer Opern von Mozart schätzt.
       that Olga always operas by Mozart appreciates
    b. *?Was_i hat Olga immer [_NP t_i für Opern] geschätzt?
       what has Olga always   for operas appreciated

The examples in (60) show that the scrambled order is perfectly grammatical with the verb *schätzen* 'appreciate', and it is in fact preferred. But the *was-für* split is quite bad in this case, just as it was in the scrambled sentence in (58b).

(60) a. ... daß Olga Opern von Mozart immer schätzt.
       that Olga operas by Mozart always appreciates
       '... that Olga always appreciates operas by Mozart.'
    b. *Was_i hat Olga [_NP t_i für Opern] immer geschätzt?
       what has Olga   for operas always appreciated

To summarize, the overall generalization seems to be that extraction is only possible from a nonscrambled (VP-internal) object NP. Since scrambling in German produces the QR reading of an indefinite object, this is parallel to the English observation: extraction from NP is not compatible with the QR (quantificational) reading of the NP. This generalization indicates that Erteschik-Shir's observations concerning "semantic dominance" can in fact be recast in terms of the theory of NP interpretation I have been developing here. Of course, there is still the question of *why* extraction and interpretation should be related. But before considering why extraction is ruled out in quantificational contexts, I now consider one more class of verbs, the so-called verbs of destruction.

4.4.8 Verbs of Destruction: *Destroy, Burn, Tear Up,* and *Ban*

The preceding discussion did not exhaustively cover the observations made by Horn (1974) and Erteschik-Shir (1973). In addition to discussing creation, using, and experiencer verbs, they claim that verbs of destruction like *destroy, burn, tear up,* and *ban* are also somewhat resistant to extraction from indefinite object NPs:

(61) a. *What did you destroy a painting of?
    b. *?Who did you burn a picture of?
    c. *What did you tear up a paper about?
    d. *Who did the school board ban a book by?

Since these verbs, unlike the experiencer verbs, are not generally considered to be individual-level predicates (and consequently we cannot assume that they are lacking a spatiotemporal argument), it is perhaps not immediately obvious why they should resist extraction, beyond the informal comments regarding an existence presupposition given in section 4.3.2. An important clue lies in the fact that the grammaticality of extraction with these verbs can vary greatly with the context.

The first thing to note here is that the sentences in (61) all involve episodic tense. In order to keep the discussion parallel to that in the previous sections, I will first discuss the generic (or habitual) contexts produced by adverbs of quantification such as *usually* and then return to the episodic cases.

As we have seen, habitual sentences are in principle ambiguous between quantificational and existential readings for indefinite objects, with the existential reading arising when the adverb of quantification binds some sort of situational variable. As we saw in the discussion of Kratzer's (1989) variable-binding facts, it is the possibility of the adverb of quantification binding some situational variable that allows the existential reading. In the absence of such a variable the adverb of quantification must bind the indefinite, or else a situation of vacuous quantification will arise.

With this in mind, one possible reason for the awkwardness of the examples in (61) is that the "once-only" nature of verbs of destruction makes binding of a temporal variable unlikely and thereby rules out the extraction-permitting existential reading. In other words, it may be that the binding of the situational variable requires that the binding be over situations—a plurality of possible situations is required (see De Swart 1991 for a similar proposal). If this is the case, the extractions in (61) should be improved by choosing habitual contexts in which the activity can be repeated, allowing quantification over a number of situations. This should enable the adverb of quantification to bind a situational variable and permit the existential reading for the object NP to be easily isolated.

In (62)–(65) I give sentences in the present tense (associated with generic/habitual interpretations; see Carlson 1977b for more discussion of tense and genericity). In conjunction with the adverb *usually* this context makes the existential reading quite plausible. Not surprisingly, extraction is also possible in this context.

(62) a. Elephants usually destroy pictures of ivory hunters.
     b. What do elephants usually destroy pictures of?

(63) a. The school board usually bans books about linguists.
     b. What does the school board usually ban books about?

(64) a. Egbert usually tears up articles about recycling.
     b. What does Egbert usually tear up articles about?

(65) a. Evelina usually burns books by Augustus F. Whipple.

b. Who does Evelina usually burn books by?

As expected, the (a) sentences in these examples are all ambiguous between a cardinal reading and a quantificational reading for the indefinite object NP. The quantificational reading disappears in the extraction sentences in the (b) examples.

The extractions in (62)–(65) all involve generic sentences with the adverb of quantification *usually*. This leaves the question of whether there is any way of biasing the *episodic* past tense toward an existential reading by creating a generic context (which can easily allow the existential interpretation) within the episodic tense. One such context would be one in which the destruction of paintings, the burning of pictures, and so on, are presented as habitual activities by means of time adverbials such as *every day*, *every week*, or *every year* (note that these adverbials explicitly bind temporal variables). Some examples of this sort are given in (66)–(69).

(66) I'm cleaning out the old paintings stored in my attic, and I try to destroy a painting of one of my more obnoxious ancestors every day.

—Who did you destroy a painting of today?

(67) Oscar burns a picture of a linguist every day.

—Who did Oscar burn a picture of yesterday?

(68) To soothe my ragged nerves, I tear up a paper about a topic related to my dissertation each week.

—What did you tear up a paper about last week?

(69) Our school board bans a book by a famous linguist every year.

—Who did the school board ban a book by this year?

In (67)–(66) activities such as picture burning and book banning are clearly presented as habitual acts (just as in sentences with *usually*). These generic contexts strongly favor the existential reading for the indefinite object. Thus, the context sentence in (67) does not mean 'Every day, if he sees a picture of a linguist, Oscar burns it'. Likewise, the context sentence in (69) does not mean that every year the school board has shown an inclination to ban *any* book by a famous linguist that came to its attention. The (simplified) logical representations for the relevant portions of the context sentences are given in (71)–(73).

(70) $\text{Every}_d \, [d \text{ is a day}] \, \exists_x \, x \text{ is a painting} \wedge I \text{ destroy } x \text{ at } d$

(71) $\text{Every}_d \, [d \text{ is a day}] \, \exists_x \, x \text{ is a picture} \wedge \text{Oscar burns } x \text{ at } d$

(72) Every$_w$ [w is a week] $\exists_x$ x is a paper $\wedge$ I tear up x in w

(73) Every$_y$ [y is a year] $\exists_x$ x is a book $\wedge$ school board bans x in y

From the representations given it can be seen that QR has not applied to the indefinite objects, since they are not introduced in the restrictive clause, but appear in the nuclear scope. This being the case, it is not surprising that extraction is possible in these environments, since extraction should be possible when QR need not apply.

Thus, even in the episodic tense it is possible to bring out a context in which extraction is possible out of objects of verbs like *destroy*. Unlike the experiencer verbs, *destroy, burn, ban*, and *tear up* do not categorically rule out extraction (and existential readings for indefinite objects); they are merely predisposed toward a nonexistential reading in certain contexts in which the "once-only action" interpretation of these verbs is the default case. Thus, in the absence of other factors that might bring out an existential reading (such as the implication of repeated actions brought out by habitual contexts), these verbs simply "select" the quantificational reading of the indefinite object.

This account of the *destroy* extraction facts (which depends on a preference for the quantificational reading of an indefinite object) also predicts that ACD should be possible with indefinite objects with these verbs, since ACD is possible when QR takes place. With most of the verbs in this class ACD is actually bad for pragmatic reasons, as shown by the following example:

(74) ?I usually destroy pictures that you do.

The sentence in (74) is odd, since it is difficult to destroy a picture in more than one situation. *Ban* does permit repetition of action and does permit ACD:

(75) The school board usually bans books that we do.

In (75) the relevant reading is that in which the adverb *usually* binds *books* rather than times. In other words, it can be paraphrased as 'The school board bans most of the books (i.e., titles) we do'. It may even be possible to devise plausible ACD contexts for *burn*:

(76) The space shuttle burns fuels that Toyotas do.

Thus, there are cases where ACD is possible with indefinite objects of verbs of destruction. This observation, along with the other data presented in this subsection, indicates that the extraction characteristics of the verbs of destruction can be explained in the same manner as the verb classes discussed above. The verbs of destruction appear to be resistant to extraction because in nonhabitual contexts they tend to prefer the quantificational reading for an indefinite object. Thus, the facts in (61) can be explained by the constraint against extracting out of an NP that must undergo QR, just as in the case of extraction out of strong NPs.

4.4.9 Verb Types and Weak Crossover

Finally, the discussion of verb types and possible interpretations leads to an interesting approach to weak crossover phenomena. The verbs of destruction are interesting in their behavior with respect to weak crossover. That certain indefinites can appear in weak crossover contexts is well known. Fodor and Sag (1982) note that one property of "specific" indefinites is that they are permitted in the weak crossover configuration. In chapter 3 I argued that "specific" indefinites should in fact be analyzed as presuppositional, or quantificational, indefinites. Thus, it is not surprising that indefinite objects of verbs like *destroy* in episodic (nonhabitual) tense are like specific (i.e., quantificational) indefinites in being able to bind a pronoun on their left without inducing weak crossover effects. As might be expected, the verbs of destruction differ in this respect from verbs of creation (which strongly disfavor a specific or quantificational reading) and are similar to the verbs of using (which readily permit the quantificational interpretation):

(77) a. Since I thought it$_i$ was offensive, I destroyed [a painting of distressed peasants]$_i$.
 b. Because I thought it$_i$ would heat the room nicely, I burned [a book about supply-side economics]$_i$.
 c. Since it$_i$ was considered to be too abstract, the school board banned [a book by Chomsky]$_i$.

(78) a. Since I thought it$_i$ was a sterling example of the Mannheim School, I played [a concerto by Karl Stamitz]$_i$.
 b. Because I was told it$_i$ was profound, I read [a book by Chomsky]$_i$.
 c. Since I thought it$_i$ was a work of art, I published [a book about dugongs]$_i$.

(79) a. *?Since I wanted to sell it$_i$, I painted [a picture of tarantulas]$_i$.
 b. *?Since I needed it$_i$ for a class, I wrote [a paper on seaweed harvesting]$_i$.
 c. *?Because I wanted to hang it$_i$ on my wall, I painted [a picture of Scottish Highland cattle]$_i$.

The sentences in (77) and (78) seem to be considerably more acceptable than those in (79). It appears that the availability of the quantificational interpretation for an indefinite licenses weak crossover.

This contrast can be explained if the indefinites in (79) (as well as (78)) are regarded as variables (as assumed by Heim (1982)). In this case the infelicitousness of the sentences in (79) is a result of a violation of the Leftness Condition of Chomsky (1976) (the Bijection Principle of Koopman and Sportiche (1982) cannot apply here, since the configuration of an operator binding two variables is not found). This is also seen in simpler examples:

(80) a. *Oscar gave their$_i$ homework papers to the students$_i$.
     b. *Olga bought his$_i$ Scottish Highland cow from a man$_i$.

The pronouns in (80) cannot be coindexed with the indefinites on their right. The question that remains is what it is about the indefinites in (77) that makes their appearance in the weak crossover configuration acceptable. To answer this question, I will first consider the crossover behavior of indefinites in general.

Although the indefinites in (80) are subject to some kind of "leftness condition," indefinites with added descriptive content are not subject to this restriction (Wasow 1979). Thus, coreference is possible in the following sentence:

(81) The donkey he$_i$ loved most kicked [a farmer I know]$_i$.

Recall that Fodor and Sag (1982) claim that "specific indefinites" such as *a farmer I know* are in fact distinct from other cases of indefinites in that they are directly referential (see section 3.4.3 for more discussion of Fodor and Sag's arguments). This would account for the acceptability of (81), since the indefinite would not in this case be a variable and thus would not be subject to any "leftness condition."

If Fodor and Sag's analysis is correct, we would expect that only referential NPs should be permitted in the object position of sentences like (81). One case where the crossover effect seems clear is that of NPs that undergo QR. In these cases, the NP raises and leaves behind a trace that functions as a variable. As shown in (82), this variable cannot bind a pronoun to its left.

(82) *The donkey who loved him$_i$ kicked every farmer$_i$.

This raises a potential problem for my explanation of the facts in (77)–(79), since my claim is that quantificational NPs are permitted in the weak crossover configuration. Notice, however, that the crossover effect disappears with the plural form of the pronoun, indicating discourse anaphora with respect to the quantificational NP:

(83) The donkey who loved them$_i$ kicked every farmer$_i$.

What I would like to suggest (continuing the line of argumentation introduced in chapter 3, contra Fodor and Sag) is that "specific" indefinites and quantified NPs are not as different with respect to weak crossover as they may at first appear. In fact, the relevant property that permits the so-called specific indefinites in weak crossover contexts is not that they are referential and thus not subject to constraints on variables such as the Leftness Condition. Rather, the "specific" indefinites behave just as quantificational NPs do in that they can license discourse anaphora (the nonreferential approach to specific indefinites is also advocated by Kripke (1977)). And it is this property that licenses the "specific" indefinites in weak crossover contexts such as (81).[22]

Thus, the behavior of the verbs of destruction in the weak crossover configuration provides additional support for the quantificational characterization of specific indefinites in chapter 3, since much of the discussion in this section has been devoted to showing that the interpretation of these objects is essentially quantificational in nature. The indefinite objects of *destroy*-type verbs pattern with quantificational NPs in that they introduce discourse anaphora, an important factor in weak crossover cases. Explaining the weak crossover facts by resorting to a referential analysis would result in losing these generalizations. Instead, the weak crossover configuration can be licensed by another property of quantificational NPs: their ability to bind the pronouns as discourse anaphora.[23]

4.4.10   Final Overview of Verb Types
I have examined a number of different classes of transitive verbs and found that they fall into roughly four classes: verbs of creation, verbs of using, experiencer verbs, and verbs of destruction. Certain syntactic properties of these verbs parallel certain preferences concerning the interpretation of indefinite objects. I distinguished two types of interpretations for indefinite NPs. One was a quantificational (or presuppositional) reading involving obligatory QR. The other was a cardinal existential reading involving existential closure, and thus no QR. The availability of the first reading correlates with the possibility of ACD and with the possibility of scrambling an indefinite object in German, and the availability of the second reading correlates with the possibility of extraction from NP.

The verbs of creation (*write, paint,* etc.) permit the existential closure reading and do not seem to allow the presuppositional reading. Consequently, extraction from NP is most felicitous with these verbs, and ACD is bad. Scrambling of an indefinite object is also not possible in German with verbs of creation.

The verbs of using (*read, play,* etc.) permit both the existential closure reading and the presuppositional reading of an indefinite object. Extraction and ACD are both acceptable with these verbs, as is German scrambling.

Experiencer verbs permit only the quantificational reading of an indefinite. ACD is fine with experiencer predicates, but extraction is ruled out. In German the scrambled order of an indefinite object is preferred with experiencer verbs.

Finally, the verbs of destruction (*burn, ban,* etc.) strongly favor a quantificational (presuppositional) reading for indefinite objects. The existential closure reading can be brought out only in habitual contexts that allow an interpretation with iterated action. Thus, in neutral episodic sentences extraction from NP is awkward with these verbs.[24]

So far I have been concerned only with pinning down the relationship between extraction and interpretation. I have not yet dealt with the question of *why* extraction from NP should be incompatible with quantifier raising of the NP. In broad intuitive terms, there seems to be a syntactic constraint against raising (via QR) an NP containing a trace. In the next section I will make a proposal relating this observation to other constraints on movement and/or representations within the Government-Binding Theory.

4.5 Formulating the Extraction Constraint

In the previous sections I examined both extraction from objects and the interpretation possibilities for indefinite objects of various verbs. I found that extractability correlates with the availability of an existential reading for an indefinite object, which in turn correlates with an inability to license discourse anaphora in the weak crossover configuration. In this section I consider the question of why extraction should depend on the possibility of the "existential closure" interpretation for an indefinite object. In this case there appears to be a constraint on extraction that must be derived from the semantico-syntactic differences between quantificational (i.e., presuppositional) and cardinal NPs.

In chapter 3 I claimed that presuppositional NPs differ from cardinal NPs in that they obligatorily undergo QR. This raising operation was associated with the process of restrictive clause formation through the tree-splitting algorithm that mapped syntactic representations into tripartite logical representations. Thus, the obligatoriness of QR with respect to presuppositional NPs follows from the existence of the presuppositions (recall that generic indefinites can in fact be regarded as presuppositional) and the operation of the process of presupposition accommodation, following ideas developed by Berman (1991). The logic of this explanation is as follows:

1. The existence presuppositions of a quantificational NP are tied to the existence of a restrictive clause (Hausser 1973, Berman 1991).
2. VPs are always mapped into nuclear scopes of tripartite quantificational structures (tree splitting).
3. Therefore, presuppositional NPs must raise out of VP before tree splitting can take place (obligatory QR).

Given this explanation, the observed prohibition on extraction from a presuppositional NP stated in the constraint in (22) can be restated as follows:

(84) *Revised Extraction Constraint*
    Extraction cannot take place out of an NP that must raise out of VP before tree splitting.

The constraint in (84) looks vaguely like the Freezing Principle of Wexler and Culicover (1980:119). The Freezing Principle roughly states that no rule can affect a node that is nonbase (e.g., a node that has been previously moved, or a node that has been affected by material moving out of it).

Wexler and Culicover state the Freezing Principle as a very general constraint, without specifying levels or deriving the restriction from more basic syntactic principles. The more limited constraint in (84) as it applies to cases of extraction from NP considered here involves a very specific situation, in which NPs containing an extraction site are adjoined to IP by either QR or scrambling. The question to be answered is whether this extraction constraint can be subsumed under any existing constraint.

The constraint in (84) basically states that moving an NP (whether by scrambling or QR) rules out *wh*-movement from that NP. Why should moving an NP have this effect? The possibility that I am going to consider here is that moving the NP creates a configuration that violates some other condition on *wh*-extraction (or the traces left by *wh*-movement). The constraint that comes most readily to mind is Subjacency, as formulated in Chomsky 1986a. Chomsky states Subjacency as a locality condition on links of a chain:[25]

(85) a. If (α_i, α_{i+1}) is a link of a chain, then α_{i+1} is 1-subjacent to α_i.
   b. β is n-subjacent to α iff there are fewer than $n + 1$ barriers for β that exclude α.

To see how Subjacency may apply in these cases, it is useful to first consider German, in which all the relevant movement (i.e., both *wh*-movement and scrambling) occurs at S-structure. Recall that the relevant generalization in German is that *was-für* extraction from an NP dominated by VP (that is, an unscrambled object) is grammatical, whereas extraction from an NP dominated by IP (such as a scrambled object NP) is bad:

(86) a. ... daß Otto immer Romane von Joseph Roth gelesen hat.
         that Otto always novels by Joseph Roth read   has
         '... that Otto has always read novels by Joseph Roth
         (e.g., before going to bed).'
   b. Was$_i$ hat [$_{IP}$ Otto immer [$_{VP}$ [$_{NP}$ t$_i$ für Romane] gelesen]]?
      what has   Otto always   for novels   read
      'What kind of novels has Otto always read?'

(87) a. ... daß Otto Romane von Joseph Roth immer gelesen hat.
         that Otto novels by Joseph Roth always read   has
         '... that Otto has always read novels by Joseph Roth = If it's a
         novel by Joseph Roth, Otto has read it.'
   b. *Was$_i$ hat [$_{IP}$ Otto [$_{IP}$[$_{NP}$ t$_i$ für Romane] immer gelesen]]?
       what has   Otto   for novels   always read

These data recall the cases of subject extractions with stage- and individual-level predicates in German that I discussed in chapter 2. As in those examples, since scrambling moves the NP to an ungoverned position, the generalization here is clearly reminiscent of Chomsky's (1986a) reformulation of Huang's (1982) Condition on Extraction Domain (CED), which prohibits movement out of ungoverned positions. To show briefly how this works in the case of the contrast between (86b) and (87b), I give the relevant definitions (with the modifications from chapter 2) from Chomsky 1986a:[26]

(88) *Barrier*
   γ is a barrier for β iff (a) or (b):
   a. γ immediately dominates δ, δ a blocking category (BC) for β;
   b. γ is a BC for β, $\gamma \neq$ IP.

(89) *Blocking category*
   γ is a BC for β iff γ is not L-marked and γ dominates β.

(90) *L-marking*
   α L-marks β iff α is a lexical category that θ-governs β. (α θ-marks β and is a sister to β)

(91) *Spec-head agreement*
   If a head L-marks a maximal projection, it L-marks the specifier of the projection. (Koopman and Sportiche 1988)

   In the case of extraction from within VP (as in (86b)), the verb L-marks NP by θ-assignment under the sisterhood relation. In this case the object NP is neither a BC nor a barrier for the trace and the extraction is grammatical. In the case of extraction from the scrambled position shown in (87b), the verb θ-marks NP, but the NP is not a sister to the verb at S-structure. Therefore, the NP is not L-marked. This leads to a Subjacency violation, since the NP is a BC (and also a barrier), and the IP is not L-marked and dominates a BC, becoming itself a barrier. Thus, the extraction in (87b) crosses two barriers and is ruled out.

   This explanation relies on two crucial assumptions concerning L-marking and barrierhood. First, although the object NP in (87b) is L-marked in its *base* (unscrambled) position, L-marking is not preserved by movement. The scrambled NP in (87b) is not L-marked. A second necessary assumption is that adjoined segments of a category must be able to inherit barrierhood (contra May 1985 and Chomsky 1986a). These two assumptions are also made by Browning (1991) to account for the ungrammaticality of extraction from topicalized constituents in English, a configuration similar to the German scrambling examples:[27]

(92) *$[_{CP}$ Who$_i$ do $[_{IP}$ you think $[_{CP}$ that $[_{IP}$ $[_{NP}$ pictures of t_i] $[_{IP}$ Bert likes]]]]]?

The topicalization operation creates an adjoined IP segment, which acts as a barrier to extraction out of the topicalized "picture" NP object.

   Finally, it should also be noted that if Subjacency were to be stated as a condition on movement rather than representations (see the discussion in Browning 1991), certain assumptions concerning rule application would have to be made. Specifically, this account requires that the scrambling operation precede *wh*-movement; otherwise, the configuration leading to the Subjacency violation would not arise.

Since the German data and the English data reduce to the same generalization—namely, that extraction is only possible from NPs that can receive an existential closure interpretation—it is natural (and desirable) to try to give a uniform explanation for the two languages. Although the explanation of the German data thus far seems relatively unproblematic, applying this explanation to the English data raises a number of problems. First, it becomes clear that Subjacency must be stated as a condition on representations, rather than a movement condition. This is simply because the ordering constraint required for a movement condition (adjunction to IP precedes *wh*-movement) cannot hold in English, since *wh*-movement at S-structure must precede QR at LF.

It is helpful at this point to go through the mechanics of the derivations of the English sentences. Recall that in English the existential closure interpretation of an NP arises from its being within the VP at the level of LF (where tree splitting takes place). The quantificational reading arises when an NP has been raised by QR out of the VP to adjoin to IP at LF. This results in the LF representations shown in (94).

(93) What does Oscar usually read books about?

(94) a. $[_{CP}$ What$_i$ does $[_{IP}$ Oscar usually $[_{VP}$ read $[_{NP}$ books about $t_i]]]]$?
    b. *$[_{CP}$ What$_i$ $[_{IP}[_{NP}$ books about $t_i]_j$ $[_{IP}$ Oscar usually $[read $t_j]]]]$?

What is interesting here is that although *wh-movement* clearly does not violate Subjacency in the representation in (94b), the end result (after QR) is that the structural relationship between the *wh*-word and its trace t_i is parallel to that in the scrambled German sentence in (87b), but at the level of LF rather than S-structure. Thus, the trace is separated from its antecedent by two barriers as a result of QR. But in this case *wh*-movement precedes QR. Therefore, any single constraint that will rule out both (87b) and (94b) must be order-independent with respect to QR and *wh*-movement. Put in another way, the constraint must be representational in nature.

A second (and perhaps more consequential) problem in formulating a Subjacency explanation for the English data is that this constraint must apply at LF as well as S-structure. Simply reformulating Subjacency as a constraint on S-structure representations (as argued in Browning 1991, for example) will not solve the problem, since in English the illicit configuration arises only at LF. Thus, an account that assimilates the Revised Extraction Constraint in (84) to Subjacency (in this case as a reformulation of Huang's CED) would require some basic modifications in the workings of Subjacency itself.[28]

The issue of whether Subjacency really should only apply at S-structure is controversial. In considering some of the arguments against having Subjacency apply at LF, it is not clear to me that this restriction to the level of S-structure is correct, even apart from the cases discussed here. If LF movement of an NP by QR can induce a Subjacency violation, then LF movement of other kinds should produce the same effect. A classic test case is that of *wh*-in-situ in English, which is assumed to involve LF movement of the *wh*-phrase (see Pesetsky 1987). The relevant cases stem from Huang's (1982) discussion of his CED, which acts as an S-structure constraint on movement, ruling out movement from ungoverned positions. The two core cases of the CED are extraction from adjuncts and extraction from subjects (the latter subsumes the Subject Condition of Ross (1967)). Huang notes that the CED does not seem to hold of LF extraction from adjuncts in English:

(95) a.   Who complained after Egbert kicked who?
     b.   *Who$_i$ did Evelina complain after Egbert kicked t$_i$?

Although the LF adjunct extraction (95a) is grammatical, as compared to the S-structure extraction in (95b), I find the cases of LF extraction corresponding to extraction from subjects to be considerably less acceptable (pace Huang 1982 and Lasnik and Saito 1992) than the adjunct extraction. The subject extraction is also less acceptable than LF extraction from objects.

(96) a.   *?Who said that friends of who kicked Egbert?
     b.   Who said that Egbert kicked friends of who?

Thus, it appears that at least the Subject Condition portion of the CED may apply at LF (this judgment is shared by Pesetsky (1982)).

Another interesting fact is that degradation of acceptability of LF *wh*-movement is not seen only with subject extractions. A number of speakers also get a contrast in LF extraction from "picture" NP objects if the determiner varies, paralleling the extraction contrasts between strong and weak NPs at S-structure noted in the discussion of the so-called specificity effects above:

(97) a.   Who said that Egbert painted a picture of who?
     b.   Who said that Egbert drew many pictures of who?
     c.   Who said that Egbert painted three pictures of who?
     d.   ??Who said that Egbert drew every picture of who?

e. *?Who said that Egbert painted the picture of who?

f. *Who said that Egbert drew most pictures of who?

Assuming that the NPs with strong determiners undergo QR at LF, the ultimate LF syntactic configurations of the sentences in (97d–f) will be similar to the one in (94b). Thus, it seems that LF *wh*-movement is subject to the same limitation with respect to quantifier phrases as S-structure *wh*-movement.[29] Allowing Subjacency to apply at LF in English yields a Subjacency-based explanation for these "specificity effects." Interestingly, this explanation accounts for the semantic nature of the extraction contrasts, through the relationship between QR and presupposition, unlike Bowers's (1988) Subjacency analysis, which involved a contrast between NP and DP.[30]

The main point that arises out of this discussion is that a Subjacency account of the extraction contrasts in both English and German will have to have two properties: (1) it will have to apply at LF as well as S-structure, and (2) it will have to be stated as a condition on representations, rather than a condition on movement.[31] The English case highlights both of these aspects. Extraction out of an NP leaves a trace within the NP. When the NP is subsequently raised to IP (at LF), two barriers then intervene between the NP-internal trace and its antecedent. Thus, unlike the CED violations, which result from (S-structure) movement taking place from a position that is not properly governed, it is the configuration that results from QR at LF moving the trace left by *wh*-movement that causes the violation of (84), not the *wh*-movement itself.

The case of extracting from an NP that must undergo QR therefore differs from the case of extracting from an NP that appears in an ungoverned position (e.g., [Spec, IP]) at S-structure:

(98) *Who were pictures of seen by John?

The CED as formulated by Huang rules out (98) by stating that *wh*-movement cannot apply to the base configuration, rather than by appealing to LF movement in the form of QR.

Additionally, suggesting that Subjacency should apply at LF does not eliminate the need for a subjacency constraint at S-structure as well. To rule out (98), it is necessary that Subjacency apply at S-structure; otherwise, the sentence could conceivably be saved by LF lowering of the subject into [Spec, VP]. Thus, LF movement can *create* a Subjacency violation, but it cannot *save* a Subjacency violation that already existed at S-structure.

The advantage of this explanation is that it accounts for a rather broad range of phenomena that share the property of being induced by presuppositionality. Not only does it explain both the German and English facts discussed above, but it also includes the contrasts in (7)–(9). The NPs that have strong determiners, or are indicated as "specific" by the combination *a certain*, must move (by QR) at LF to be incorporated into a restrictive clause. This movement rules out any possibility of S-structure extraction out of the NP, since such movement would result in the NP (and the trace within) being raised by the subsequent obligatory application of QR to a position that brings about a violation of Subjacency.

The possibility of extraction in the case of certain NPs with "definite" determiners is also explained by this account. An example of such a case is the indefinite use of *this*:

(99) a. There's this cow that I see every morning.
     b. There's this cow that Egbert is painting this wonderful picture of.

These NPs are nonquantificational, as shown by their ability to appear in *there*-sentences such as (99a). Therefore, NPs with the indefinite *this* do not need to undergo QR. Thus, this sort of demonstrative NP will remain in situ at LF, the NP-internal trace will not be moved to a position that will yield a Subjacency violation, and extractions such as (99b) are perfectly grammatical.

Of course, referential NPs such as names, pronouns, and demonstratives are presuppositional as well, and they behave as such in *there*-insertion constructions. It is not supposed here that these NPs undergo QR, but since they NPs do not take complements from which extraction could occur, the nonapplicability of the QR-based account of extraction is irrelevant.

Additionally, this conception of Subjacency may also explain the facts noted in chapter 3 concerning extraposition. Recall that extraposition is less acceptable from NPs with strong determiners:

(100) a. A review appeared of *The Joy of Cooking*.
      b. Many reviews appeared of *The Joy of Cooking*.
      c. *Every review appeared of *The Joy of Cooking*.
      d. *Most reviews appeared of *The Joy of Cooking*.

Assuming (contra Baltin 1987) that extraposition leaves a trace, adjunction to IP of the quantificational NPs in (100c) and (100d) will leave the trace of extraposition in a position where it is separated from its antecedent by two intervening barriers. "Weak" NPs, which do not need to undergo QR, will not bring about this problem, leading to the contrast between the two types of NPs seen in (100).[32]

A final point in favor of the presupposition-based analysis concerns the nature of the judgments themselves. As I noted above, the data discussed in this chapter are notoriously vague. The judgments concerning extraction from NPs are extremely uncertain and can easily be "pushed" in one direction or the other. Given the role that presence or absence of presuppositionality plays in determining the acceptability of extraction, this is not surprising. The vagueness in judgments arises from the fact that the acceptability of extraction hinges on the availability of the existential closure interpretation for the NP in question. Distinguishing this reading from the presuppositional ("specific") existential reading can be very difficult, leading to the difficulty in making sharp distinctions in grammaticality. The most problematic case is the class of verbs of destruction, in which the existential closure reading of the indefinite is possible only in habitual contexts, and not in neutral episodic sentences.

Contrary to what is empirically observed, the analyses of Bowers (1988) and Horn (1974) predict fairly sharp judgments. Bowers's account predicts that all weak NPs should permit extraction, whereas no strong NPs should. Horn's account predicts that all verbs that show evidence of structural ambiguity with "picture" noun objects should permit extraction, whereas those that do not show ambiguity should not. Both of these ways of accounting for the extraction facts are too rigid. They do not account for the fact that the judgments are not always clear, and that they are frequently context dependent. According to the explanation I have given for these phenomena (following the lead of Erteschik-Shir (1973) in acknowledging the importance of presupposition), this vagueness is actually an expected characteristic of the judgments, rather than an inconvenient complication.

4.6 Concluding Remarks

To sum up the results of this chapter and the monograph as a whole: I initially proposed a procedure (the Mapping Hypothesis, or tree-splitting algorithm) by which logical representations of the sort developed by Kamp (1981) and Heim (1982) can be derived from syntactic representations of sentence. This procedure involves a simple division of a syntactic tree into two parts, corresponding to the restrictive clause and nuclear scope of the Kamp-Heim representations.

More detailed investigation of the workings of the procedure and also the possible interpretations of NPs (drawing on the work of Milsark (1974)) led to a more complex classification of indefinites than that originally proposed by Kamp and Heim. Indefinites were found to be distinguished by two features: whether or not they have quantificational force, and whether or not they obligatorily undergo QR. The Mapping Hypothesis was given further support by an asymmetry in the semantic and syntactic properties of the subjects of two particular types of predicates, the stage- and individual-level predicates of Carlson (1977b).

I also examined a number of transitive verb types and found that verbs vary in which interpretations (e.g., either a QR reading or a non-QR reading) they prefer (or even allow) for indefinite objects. This variation was linked to the possibility of extracting from "picture" noun objects of various kinds occurring with the different types of verbs. An incompatibility was found between *wh*-movement and QR, in the sense that extraction is not possible out of an NP that must undergo QR. Comparison of German (which has an S-structure scrambling rule that has a semantic effect similar to that of LF QR in English) and English revealed that this constraint holds regardless of the ordering of *wh*-movement and the "QR" rule. This observation led to a formulation of Subjacency that allows a level-independent account of the extraction facts.

Notes

Chapter 1

1. Pollock (1989) expands upon this structure, positing additional inflectional heads, rather than a single unitary Infl(ection) node. Although the semantics of these additional syntactic positions remains to be explicated, in this work I have not taken advantage of the possibilities opened up by this approach, leaving it as a matter for further research.

2. I will not present detailed argumentation for the existence of the level of LF, although the issue has been the subject of a fair amount of consideration in recent works. See May 1985, 1988, Williams 1977, 1986, 1988, and Pesetsky 1987 for some representative discussion.

3. I include Kamp's notation for expository purposes only. Though it may be intuitively easier to grasp than the more conventional notation, it is for all other purposes equivalent.

4. If the restrictive clause is not satisfied by the number of variable assignments required by the quantifier, then the truth-conditions of the sentence may be either false or undefined. Since nothing discussed here hinges on the choice between these two options, I will for convenience refer to the truth-value in these cases as undefined.

5. Restricted quantifier analysis does not originate with Kamp and Heim. An early formulation of restricted quantification is found in Hailperin 1957, with some early natural language applications in Bacon 1965 and Hausser 1973.

It is also worth noting here that one major advantage of using restricted quantification for analyzing natural language quantification is that it permits the representation of quantifiers such as *most* and *few*, which are inherently relational (e.g., in the sentence *Most pigs oink*, the number of things that are pigs is compared with the size of the subset of pigs that oink, giving a proportion), and cannot be modeled with standard first-order predicate calculus and truth-functional connectives (Barwise and Cooper 1981).

6. Not all accounts of extraction islands are derivational. There are a number of researchers who argue for a representational approach to island effects, such

as Freidin (1978), Kayne (1984), Koster (1978, 1987), McDaniel (1989), and Browning (1991).

Chapter 2

1. Farkas and Sugioka (1983) also utilize a generic operator in analyzing *if/when* clauses.

2. The terms *stage* and *individual* refer to particular elements of Carlson's ontology. Although I neither adopt his analysis nor make use of his ontology, I retain his terminology since it has become commonly used in the semantic literature.

3. The conclusions I reach with regard to the distribution of readings differ somewhat from those of Carlson (1977b). Carlson assumes that stage-level *adjectival* predicates such as *available* allow only an existential reading, whereas individual-level adjectival predicates allow only the generic reading. At first glance, the examples in (i) seem to confirm this.

(i) a. Pigs are available. (existential only)
    b. Pigs are intelligent. (generic only)

I think that in fact the generic reading in (ia) is ruled out pragmatically. Although it is not unreasonable to expect that firemen might have a generic property of being available, in the actual world it is quite odd to expect the same of pigs. Thus, the following sentence involving the stage-level predicate *is visible* is clearly ambiguous between the existential and generic readings:

(ii) Pigs are visible.

See Diesing 1988 for a more in-depth discussion of the contrasts between the sort of analysis proposed here and the one proposed in Carlson 1977b.

4. I will discuss the interpretation of other types of NPs in chapter 3.

5. As the literature concerning "derived subjects" attests, there are many ways of representing the "lower" subject position. In addition to the [Spec, VP] hypothesis I have utilized in (7), other proposals include these: the lower subject position is adjoined to VP (Koopman and Sportiche 1985, Speas 1990); the lower subject is the specifier of AgrP (e.g., external to VP, as suggested in Pollock 1989); the lower subject is adjoined to V' (Fukui and Speas 1986); the lower subject is dominated by v^{max}, but attached to the *right* of the object (Kitagawa 1986). I will not deal directly with the question of deciding among these various alternatives. The association of the lower subject position with the operation of existential closure (which extends over the VP, as I have stated it) suggests that the choice be at least narrowed down to VP-internal positions. This is admittedly a theory-dependent decision, and a closer examination of the existential closure operation and its relation to other operators such as tense (as well as any number of other considerations) could lead to another conclusion. I will leave this issue open for now and continue to represent the lower subject as [Spec, VP].

6. This proposal also requires that in cases where LF lowering of the subject into VP can occur, the subject θ-role must be assigned to the [Spec, VP] position, in a manner similar to that suggested by Kitagawa (1986).

7. An alternative to the empty expletive approach to dealing with the trace left by LF lowering would be to utilize some form of "chain binding" as proposed by Barss (1986) for cases of reconstruction. Since nothing hinges on the choice between the two approaches, I will leave the issue open.

8. Kratzer does not necessarily intend for her spatiotemporal argument to be taken as exactly equivalent to the event argument proposed by Davidson (1967).

9. Thanks are due to David Pesetsky for suggesting this line of argumentation to me.

10. Note that Fukui (1986) also allows for the generation of PRO in a VP-internal subject position, but he assumes that PRO in this position is not governed.

11. The stage-level *be* is similar, but not identical, to Partee's (1977) "active *be*." The active *be* occurs in the progressive form (in a sequence *be being*) and requires an agentive subject:

(i) a. Ernie is being noisy.
    b. *This sonata is being difficult.

12. Alternatively, the contrast between stage- and individual-level adjectives could be represented as a difference in the argument structure of the adjectives themselves (see Moltmann 1989).

13. There is still the problem of accounting for contrasts between stage- and individual-level predicates in constructions in which there is no copula, such as absolute constructions (Stump 1985) and complements of perception verbs:

(i) a. Available, Harry leapt to assist the old lady crossing the street.
    b. Under the table, the cat is safe from the dog.
    c. *Intelligent, Horace finished the test before anyone else in the class.
    d. *Six feet tall, Hilda is unable to fit under the piano.

(ii) a. Max heard Marvin in the shower.
     b. Millie saw a fireman available.
     c. *Matilda saw Max intelligent.
     d. *Marvin heard Melinda overweight.

14. This parallel does not imply that there is any correlation between the modal control structures and the individual-level control structures, or between the modal and stage-level manifestations of the raising structures. In fact, both the root and epistemic interpretations of modals can occur with both the existential and generic interpretations of bare plurals:

(i) a. Firemen must be available.
    b. Opera singers must know Hittite.

The sentence in (ia), where a stage-level predicate cooccurs with a modal, has four readings. Two are existential: an epistemic existential ('The lights are on in the fire station, firemen must be available') and a root (deontic) existential ('In order for the town to qualify for state funds, firemen must be available'). The sentence also has two generic readings: a deontic generic (being available is a required characteristic in firemen) and an epistemic generic ('Surely firemen (of all people) must be available'). The sentence in (ib), with an individual-level predicate, has only the two generic readings.

15. Having the contrast hinge on the nature of the Infl involved raises the question of what component of Infl is relevant to this contrast, especially in light of recent accounts of clause structure that make use of articulated inflectional heads, following the lead of Pollock (1989). Since there are contrasts between the two types of predicates with infinitival clauses (briefly discussed in note 17), this suggests that it may not be tense that is relevant. The contrast may therefore turn on properties of Agr.

16. This reading is sometimes thought to require an accent on the verb *hate* (Manfred Krifka, personal communication). Although it is true that such a focus pattern will force the generic reading of the object, I think that the intended reading can also arise quite easily with neutral focus, as in the following context:

(i) Q: Why don't cellists like to play Pachelbel?
     A: For one thing, cellists hate boring bass lines.

The effects of focus on NP interpretation will be discussed more extensively in a later section.

17. This raises the question of how small clause complements are to be interpreted. If the VP is the domain of existential closure, it is expected that bare plurals within small clauses would be "caught" by existential Closure and given an existential reading. This is not always the case. The existential reading does not seem to be available for subjects of small clause complements of *consider*:

(i) a. I consider firemen available. (generic only)
    b. I consider firemen intelligent. (generic only)

Exceptional case making (ECM) verbs seem more or less to allow both existential and generic interpretations of complement subjects:

(ii) a.   I believe firemen to be available. (both generic and existential)
     b.   I believe violists to be intelligent. (generic only)
     c.   ??I believe opera singers to know Hittite.

For-clauses also allow both readings:

(iii) a. For firemen to be available is the least we should expect. (ambiguous)
      b. For violists to be intelligent is the least we should expect. (generic)

With-clauses, on the other hand, do not seem to permit a generic reading, and they are generally bad with individual-level predicates:

(iv) a.   With firemen available, we are well protected against immolation.
     b.   *With firemen intelligent, we have nothing to fear.

Though I have no explanation at this point for this range of variation, the possibility of generic readings points to a clausal constituent structure for the complement in (i) (Chomsky 1981, Stowell 1981, Safir 1983; contra Williams 1983), resulting in an embedded tripartite logical representation.

18. I restrict myself to embedded contexts to avoid complications brought about by the application of the verb-second constraint. Specifically, unlike subject raising to [Spec, IP] in German, topicalization to [Spec, CP] seems to always permit "reconstruction effects" in the interpretation of the topicalized elements.

19. It may appear from this description that the split-topic construction is actually a case of quantifier floating, as analyzed by Sportiche (1988). But quantifier floating in German and split topics actually have rather different properties. One major difference is that split topics *only* arise by topicalization in conjunction with verb-second word order, whereas quantifier floating can occur in non-verb-second clauses in conjunction with scrambling. See Fanselow 1987 and Giusti 1990 for more discussion of the properties of German quantifier floating.

20. Koopman and Sportiche (1988) make a similar assumption with respect to government: "if an X^0 governs a YP, it governs the Specifier of YP" (p. 16). See also Bonet 1989 for a discussion of case assignment to [Spec,VP] via a similar mechanism. One potential problem with this extension of Spec-head agreement is that this predicts that extraction from an ECM subject should be acceptable (as claimed by Chomsky), which is debatable:

(i) a. ?Who do you believe pictures of to be on sale?
    b. *Who are pictures of on sale?

Although I believe that there is a contrast between (ia) and (ib), the acceptability of (ia) is somewhat degraded.

21. This raises the question of why L-marking should matter after *LF* lowering for a movement relation established at S-structure. I will discuss this question in detail in chapter 4.

22. This fact is pointed out by Moltmann (1991) as evidence against the hypothesis that the relevant factor in determining the acceptability of extraction is the stage/individual contrast.

23. Thanks to David Pesetsky for encouraging such flights of imagination.

24. A third question is how to represent the narrow "contrastive" focus on subject NPs such as in (75a). For present purposes, it is enough to assume that we need to distinguish two types of focus: contrastive and presupposition-inducing (contrary to Rooth 1991). Only the presupposition-inducing focus constructions are to be represented in tripartite logical representations of the sort derived by tree splitting. Thus, the contrastive cases do not bear on the viability of the Mapping Hypothesis.

Chapter 3

1. Partee (1978) and Cooper (1979) discuss similar problems in the interpretation of pronouns. See also Neale 1990 for a more recent examination of these issues.

2. The question of exactly *how* the E-type pronouns acquire the necessary descriptive content is a tricky one. I will not attempt to answer this question here, but will simply refer the reader to the discussions of this matter in Kadmon 1987 and Heim 1990.

3. I am ignoring for the moment sentences that contain a quantificational adverb. These sentences will be considered in detail in chapter 4.

4. The presuppositionality described by Milsark seems to correspond to what Soames (1989) calls "pragmatic presupposition," which can be thought of as what is taken for granted by speakers and hearers in a conversation.

5. The literature contains numerous discussions of the semantics of weak and strong determiners. In the framework of "generalized quantifiers" these include (to give a very abbreviated selection): Barwise and Cooper 1981, De Jong and Verkuyl 1985, and Partee 1988. Within the context of Government-Binding Theory, they include (among others) Higginbotham 1987 and Reinhart 1987.

6. For present purposes, I will make do with this rough characterization. A more complete account of partitivity would require some refinements. For example, De Hoop (1990) claims that a partitive characterization is not correct for strong determiners in Dutch. Her objection is based on the fact that partitives can occur in *er*-insertion sentences in Dutch:

(i) Er   zitten twee van de drie katten in de tuin.
    there sit   two of the three cats   in the garden

The occurrence of the partitive in an existential sentence may be limited to matrix (verb-second) environments, however. At least for some speakers, in embedded contexts the partitive in an existential is less acceptable (Hotze Rullmann, personal communication):

(ii) *?... dat er   twee van de drie katten in de tuin   zitten.
          that there two of the three cats   in the garden sit

Thus, the Dutch data may well involve a syntactic difference between verb-second existentials and non-verb-second existentials rather than a cross-linguistic difference in the semantic characterization of the strong determiners.

Comorovski (1989) also discusses some cases in English where partitive NPs can occur in existential sentences with codas, and concludes that there are two factors at stake: the determiner involved and the "novelty" of the NP. In cases where the NP is novel, a partitive NP can occur in an existential sentence regardless of the determiner:

(iii) There are all of yesterday's exams to correct.

If the partitive phrase is somehow anaphoric to some element of the preceding discourse, only a weak determiner is allowed in the partitive NP:

(iv) How many papers have you graded today?
     There are still some/*most of them to grade.

This phenomenon is limited to existentials with codas, however, and it is interesting to note that De Hoop's examples also all involve existential sentences with codas.

7. This description is somewhat simplified, since May 1977 and May 1985 differ in how relative scope is assigned, but that difference is not relevant to the discussion here.

8. One exception to this generalization is the analysis proposed by Hornstein (1984). Hornstein distinguishes three types of quantifiers on the basis of movement and binding considerations. His distinctions do not take into account the differences between strong and weak quantifiers, which all (with the exception of *any*) fall into the same class in his analysis.

9. A potential problem with regarding existential quantifiers as cardinality predicates was pointed out to me by Maria Bittner. The problem arises with quantifiers

like *at most three*. These are weak quantifiers in the sense that they can occur in *there*-sentences:

(i) There are at most three piglets in the yard.

Analyzing *at most three* as a cardinality predicate in (i) can result in the wrong truth-conditions, for the sentence will be true even if there are five piglets in the yard, since there will exist a set of piglets whose cardinality is at most three. What is required here is a stipulation that the set denoted by the cardinality predicate be a maximal set, somewhat along the lines of the "scalar implicature" of Horn (1972) (see also Grice 1975). This problem is discussed in more detail by Kadmon (1987) and May (1989).

10. In arguing against Diesing 1988 and Kratzer 1989, De Hoop and De Swart (1990) claim that the "strong partitive interpretations" of indefinites with weak determiners (or the presuppositional readings, as I refer to them) cannot be explained by a Kamp-Heim-style variable analysis. They are assuming a uniform analysis of indefinites, however, so their objections in this regard in fact do not hold.

11. At this point for the sake of simplicity I will assume that the quantifier is a determiner, as in all the examples considered so far in this chapter. I will deal with adverbs of quantification and the generic operator in chapter 4.

12. The connection between presupposition and restrictive clause formation was also noted by Hausser (1973). As Berman points out, this effect of presuppositions of the sentence on the logical representation has been noted elsewhere in tne literature as well—for example, by Belnap (1970) with regard to conditionals, and by Schubert and Pelletier (1989) with regard to generic sentences.

13. Of course, an indefinite taking the presuppositional reading will show a preference for wider scope. The significance of this fact will be discussed when I take up the issue of the so-called specific indefinites.

14. It must be mentioned in this connection that Carlson's (1977b) observations about the bare plural suggest that bare plurals can *never* have a wide scope (e.g., QRed) interpretation. In the account of the interpretation of bare plurals developed in chapter 2 this need not be the case, and in chapter 4 I discuss a number of instances where bare plurals do in fact seem to undergo QR.

15. In a subsequent work May (1985) proposes that both readings of (12) should be given a single representation at LF, with the two readings being derived indirectly from the LF representation. It is not clear to me how this approach could be modified to take into account the effects of the presuppositionality contrast.

16. It is of course important to bear in mind that these representations are an abbreviated form of the derivation (see the discussion in chapter 1). In particular, Heim's (1982) rule of Quantifier Construal is crucial to ensuring that the operators match up properly with their restrictive clauses.

17. This association of acts of creating with the nonpresuppositional reading will be considered in more detail in chapter 4.

18. Carlson actually characterizes the distinction in terms of a contrast between ordinary restrictive relatives and what he calls "amount relatives." The amount

relatives (which correspond to the cases involving presuppositional NPs) differ from restrictive relatives in that they contain a quantifier phrase containing a strong NP, paralleling the analysis of comparatives in Bresnan 1973.

19. Given that weak quantifiers are ambiguous, it might be expected that the sentences in (26) would be grammatical, but only allowing the presuppositional reading for the determiner. This is in fact true for some speakers. Other speakers seem to find the ACDs in (26) awkward, which may be related to the oft-noted asymmetry between subjects and objects with respect to preference for a presuppositional reading. Subjects are strongly presuppositional, whereas objects favor nonpresuppositional readings.

Tense can also affect which reading arises most readily. For example, the present perfect seems to induce a presuppositional reading:

(i) a. I have read many books that you have.
    b. I have read two books that you have.

Both of the sentences in (i) give rise to the presuppositional reading of the object quite easily, in contrast to the examples given in the text.

20. A fact left unexplained by this analysis is that comparatives are quite acceptable in ACD contexts:

(i) I read more books than you did.

The simplest approach would be to assume that comparatives require a QR (presuppositional) interpretation. It is not obvious how this would work, however. The comparative in (i) seems to clearly be comparing expressions of cardinality (i.e, the number of books read). The object NP is presuppositional in the sense that it is presupposed that books were read. I leave the question of how to incorporate the interpretation of comparatives into the account I have presented for further research.

21. It is not clear to me how Baltin derives the correct semantic interpretation of these sentences. There still seems to be a problem in recovering the deleted VP.

22. This difference between extraposition structures and ACDs was pointed out to me by Roger Higgins.

23. For some speakers extraposition from a strong NP may not be so bad as is indicated by the starred examples, although even these speakers find a contrast in that the unextraposed version is preferable.

24. Hasegawa (1988) presents arguments based on constituency tests that also show, independently of the considerations I have presented, that Baltin's extraposition analysis does not correctly derive the ACD structures.

25. The relevance of these facts to my analysis was pointed out to me by Robert May.

26. Hirschbühler (1982) raises some counterexamples to Sag's and Williams's generalization. In the following examples of VP-deletion the object NP quantified with *each* can take wider scope than the NP in subject position:

(i) A Canadian flag was hanging in front of each window, and an American one was too.
(ii) A kitty was sleeping in each corner, and a puppy was too.

These sentences seem to indicate that it is necessary for the quantified objects to raise to IP in order to take scope over their subjects. If this is so, then reconstruction of the deletion should not yield well-formedness, since an unbound variable will result. A reordering solution (in which VP-reconstruction would precede QR) would leave us without a satisfactory account of ACD, since in the case of ACD recovering of the deleted VP depends on the *prior* occurrence of QR. Hirschbühler's solution is to simply allow *each* to take scope over both conjuncts:

(iii) [each corner$_i$ [$_{IP}$ a kitty was [$_{VP}$ sleeping in t$_i$]] and [$_{IP}$ a puppy was
       [$_{VP}$ sleeping in t$_i$]]]

This special treatment would also have to be extended to *every*, since wide scope is possible with objects quantified by *every* in these contexts as well:

(iv) A kitty was sleeping in every corner, and a puppy was too.

The question, then, is whether sentences such as these are in fact a special case of some sort (perhaps due to special properties of *each*), or whether the wide scope reading can be accounted for by some more general means.

In examining both Sag's and Williams's examples on the one hand, and Hirschbühler's examples on the other, one important distinguishing characteristic comes to light. In the cases of VP-deletion where the object NP seems to be limited to narrow scope, the subject of the second conjunct is always a definite NP or a proper name:

(v) a. Some bassoonist played every sonata, but Otto didn't.
    b. Every lawyer liked some decisions, but the doctor didn't.

The subject NP in the second conjunct in the examples in (v) is arguably non-quantificational, in the sense that it does not exhibit scope interactions . Thus, the reason no across-the-board scope operations are possible in these examples may well simply be that they do not involve across-the-board quantification.

If this is the case, then VP-deletion sentences that involve quantificational (or for that matter, indefinite) NPs in both conjuncts should permit the across-the-board scope phenomena observed by Hirschbühler. This does in fact seem to be the case:

(vi) a. Donkeys kicked every farmer and goats did too.
     b. Bassoonists played every cantata and cellists did too.
     c. Frogs jumped most fences and sheep did too.
     d. Guinea pigs rode many trains and chinchillas did too.

(vii) a. Every donkey kicked three of the farmers and several goats did too.
      b. Two of the bassoonists played in every cantata and three of the cellists
         did too.
      c. Every frog jumped several fences and most sheep did too.
      d. Many guinea pigs rode every train and several chinchillas did too.

The sentences in (vi) and (vii) all seem to be ambiguous between wide and narrow scope for the object NPs. This is true of both strong NPs and weak NPs.

The question remains how the wide-scope-object readings are to be represented without resulting in the unbound variable problem. I'm not sure how to formalize this at this point, and I will leave it as a problem for further research.

27. Note that the relation of "not included in" is not equivalent to "excluded." Exclusion is defined within the *Barriers* framework as the following:

(i) α *excludes* β if and only if no segment of α dominates β.

28. Allowing QR to adjoin VPs of course raises the possibility that the narrow scope presuppositional reading discussed in sections 3.2.5 and 3.2.6 is actually a result of adjunction to VP rather than IP. This may well be correct, but I will not pursue the possibility here.

29. The presuppositional reading can also reflect a more generalized application of presupposition accommodation in that the two cellists could be members of a presupposed set of musicians, rather than specifically cellists. In this case the additional presuppositions accommodated (that there is a set of musicians, and that cellists are musicians) are represented either abstractly (as in the case of the *I have stopped eating Brussels sprouts* example) or explicitly in the preceding discourse.

30. Strictly speaking, the particles act as only a partial diagnostic of the phrase structure position of the subject. Although the appearance of a subject to the *left* of the particles clearly indicates that the subject is in [Spec, IP], a subject to the *right* of the particles may be VP-external owing to the possibility of their scrambling and adjoining to IP (this possibility was also mentioned in chapter 2). The interpretation that results in this case is rather marked, and requires a particular intonation contour. With neutral intonation, only the VP-internal (existential closure) interpretation of the indefinite is possible. This of course does not rule out the syntactic characterization of the contrast, but merely indicates that there can be other factors involved as well.

31. There has also been a fair amount of diversity in the work on specificity that has been devoted to characterizing specificity in terms of particular semantic properties. For example, specificity has been described in terms of scope and referentiality (Fodor and Sag 1982, Partee 1972), "force" versus "sense" (Higginbotham 1987), Pesetsky's (1982) notion of "D-linking" (Enç 1991), and Donnellan's (1966) contrast between referential and attributive NPs (Moltmann 1991).

32. As noted by De Mey (1980), there are a number of additional factors that can come into play in determining interpretations of bare plurals in Dutch, which I will make no attempt to account for here. For example, tense plays a role in the interpretation of bare plurals in Dutch, just as it does in English. In addition, De Mey notes that quantificational variability can also arise in the presence of quantificational adverbs for both bare plural subjects and objects. I will discuss this sort of variability in English and German in chapter 4. It appears that much of that discussion may apply to the Dutch facts as well.

33. Of course, one could construct some sort of bizarre context in which being on the roof would be a generic property of cows that could conceivably result in grammaticality, but for the purposes of this illustration I will stick with the more usual sorts of situations involving cows and roofs.

34. Bennis (1986: 254, fn. 18) makes a similar point using coreference tests of the type discussed by Reinhart (1983). He notes that definite pronouns may refer to

presuppositional (VP-external) indefinites, but not to VP-internal (existential closure) indefinites:

(i) a. De leraar wilde   dat een jongen een meisje kuste, maar hij weigerde.
        the teacher wanted that a boy   a girl   kissed but he refused

  b. *De leraar wilde   dat er   een jongen een meisje kuste, maar hij
       the teacher wanted that there a boy   a girl   kissed but he
       weigerde.
       refused

35. Rullmann (1989) considers the possibility that the Dutch specific indefinites are actually referential expressions, along the lines proposed by Fodor and Sag (1982), but does not reach a conclusive decision in this matter. I discuss Fodor and Sag's analysis in section 3.5.

36. Reuland actually describes the ambiguity of the indefinite NPs in terms of an NP-internal syntactic distinction as well. He claims that in the case of the presuppositional reading the specifier is interpreted as a determiner in the sense of Barwise and Cooper (1981), whereas in the case of the existential reading the specifier does not function as a determiner. A number of researchers have approached the ambiguity of weak determiners from the point of view of NP-internal syntax (see, for example, Bowers 1988 and Hudson 1989). This approach certainly deserves further attention, especially in light of expanded notions of NP structure due to Brame (1981) and Abney (1987), but I will leave the matter for future research at this point.

37. Morphological case marking (or the absence thereof) on direct objects produces alternations in semantic interpretations in a number of languages. Among these are Hindi (Mahajan 1990), Russian (Babby 1980, Pesetsky 1982, and Neidle 1988), and Finnish (Vainikka 1988, 1989). There is also a discussion of related phenomena regarding specificity in Hungarian in Szabolcsi 1986. Although the semantic effects of case marking vary among these languages (for example, in some instances aspect plays a role in determining the interpretation of an NP), the phenomena do seem to be related to the facts discussed by Enç (1991). Belletti (1988) has proposed an account of "definiteness effects" that is based on the distinction between structural and inherent case, motivated in part by the case distinctions in Finnish. Although there are problems with this approach to (in)definiteness (see, for example, Vainikka 1988), this is clearly an area that calls for more research.

38. Bare object NPs generally appear without case marking. One interesting exception is that of animate bare NPs. Erguvanli (1984:19) notes that in "statements of general truth" a bare animate NP must be marked with accusative case:

(i) a. Ben insanlar-ı   severim.
        I   human beings-ACC, like
        'I like human beings.'

  b. *Ben insanlar   severim.
       I   human beings like

This is clearly a case of a generic interpretation of the object of an experiencer verb, a phenomenon that was discussed briefly in chapter 2. The fact that bare objects that have morphological case marking are interpreted generically is not surprising, since generics are also associated with restrictive clause formation. This fact (as well as the Dutch bare plural facts discussed in the previous section) may lead one to think that the association between presuppositionality and accusative case marking is not correct, since generics seem nonpresuppositional. In chapter 4 I discuss the issue of presuppositionality and generics and conclude (following an argument by Angelika Kratzer) that generics can indeed be regarded as presuppositional. Therefore, I will continue to regard the notion of presuppositionality as the correct generalization in these cases.

39. Another possible approach would be to regard the casemarker itself as being a strong determiner (D) (which would trigger QR) within the DP theory of NP syntax developed by Abney (1987). This is not so unreasonable as it might first seem, since Turkish is essentially a head-final language, and D, as head of the DP, could plausibly appear phrase-finally in the NP. See Tateishi 1989 for the suggestion that morphological case markers head DPs in Japanese.

40. Ludlow and Neale also note that it is not true that universally quantified NPs cannot escape "scope islands" induced by propositional attitude verbs because the reading where the NP *every Gila monster in New Mexico* takes narrow scope with respect to *a man in Arizona*, but wide scope with respect to *thinks*, is possible:

(i) a. A man in Arizona thinks that every Gila monster in New Mexico won the
     lottery.
   b. $\exists_x$ [x is a man] Every$_y$ [y is a Gila monster] x thinks that y won the lottery

Chapter 4

1. The discussion here is based on a February, 1990 class handout of Angelika Kratzer's entitled "Some Comments on Enç," which is actually an overview of the various properties of different kinds of indefinites and their interpretations inspired by an early version of Enç 1991.

2. Generic sentences like those in (4), as well as definitional sentences like *A unicorn has one horn* are viewed as a problem for the presuppositional approach to determiner semantics by a number of researchers, including Lappin and Reinhart (1988). They do not consider the possibility of exploiting a modal approach to genericity, however.

3. I have no explanation for why there is an increase in acceptability with the plural definite in (8e).

4. Hestvik (1990) claims that Fiengo and Higginbotham's specificity distinction is actually due to the fact that specific NPs are complete functional complexes (CFCs; see also Chomsky 1986b), whereas nonspecific NPs are not. Hestvik makes this claim in a discussion of binding principles, in which he suggests that the binding domain for x is the minimal CFC containing x. In support of this, he notes the following contrast:

(i) a. *John$_i$ saw a picture of him$_i$.
   b. John$_i$ saw those pictures of him$_i$.

I feel that the contrast is weak (I'm inclined to feel that both are OK); but if there is a contrast, the strong/weak split falls along the same lines:

(ii) a. ?John$_i$ saw many pictures of him$_i$.

    b. ?John$_i$ saw three pictures of him$_i$.   *weak*

    c. John$_i$ saw every picture of him$_i$.

    d. John$_i$ saw each picture of him$_i$.   *strong*

5. The idea that in nominal constructions there is a higher level of structure (the DP) that takes NP as its complement is due to Brame (1981). This idea is also utilized by Hellan (1986) and is developed most thoroughly by Abney (1987). The DP Hypothesis is also utilized to distinguish strong and weak NPs by Hudson (1989), De Hoop (1990), and Zwarts (1990). Additionally, Stowell (1989) distinguishes between DPs and NPs as referential (DP) and nonreferential (NP). The idea of distinguishing two determiner positions for strong and weak determiners actually predates the DP Hypothesis. Jackendoff (1977) distinguishes the two classes of determiners in terms of being attached to the NP at different bar levels, and this idea is also taken up by Rothstein (1988).

6. The idea that quantifiers might be grouped into categorially distinct classes is not new. The issue is discussed in Jespersen 1927. More recent discussion can be found in Selkirk 1970, 1977 and Jackendoff 1968, 1977. Carlson (1978) gives a historical account that shows that the quantifiers in Old English all functioned as adjectives, and that the strong quantifiers have since undergone a category change.

7. The determiner interpretation of weak quantifiers would have to be forced in the case of partitives, since as I noted in chapter 3, this is one case where the presuppositional reading of weak determiners is obligatory:

(i) a. *?Who did you see many of the pictures of?

    b. *?Who did you read three of the books about?

    c. *?Who did you paint several of the pictures of?

Bowers does not discuss the structure of partitives (see Selkirk 1970 and 1977 for some discussion, as well as Jackendoff 1977), and it is conceivable that the facts in (i) could be accommodated by his analysis in some way.

8. An empirical point that might be used to support a categorial ambiguity for weak determiners like *many* is the fact that in German *viel* ('many') can show both weak and strong inflection (e.g., *viel Wein* vs. *vieler Wein*). See Olsen 1989 for an analysis of strong and weak adjective inflection in German in the context of the DP Hypothesis.

9. Horn gives three arguments for his Structural Ambiguity Hypothesis (SAH). The first involves passive formation. In the case of *write*, a sentence with a "picture" NP object actually has two passives:

(i) a. Oscar wrote a book about manatees.

    b. A book about manatees was written by Oscar.

    c. A book was written about manatees by Oscar.

In (ib) the entire NP *a book about manatees* has been fronted. In (ic) only the NP portion *a book* has moved. Assuming that (i) is structurally ambiguous, parallel to (17), the passive in (ib) can be derived from the PP-within-NP structure in (17b), and the sentence in (ic) can be derived from the PP-attached-to-VP structure in (17c).

In the case of *destroy*, however, only one passive form is possible:

(ii) a. Oscar destroyed a book about manatees.
   b. A book about manatees was destroyed by Oscar.
   c. *A book was destroyed about manatees by Oscar.

If the two passive forms are derived as described above, the ungrammaticality of (iic) suggests that the PP-attached-to-VP structure is not available in the case of *destroy*.

The second argument involves pronominalization. Horn notes that it is generally not possible to pronominalize the head noun in an NP containing modifiers:

(iii) *I saw the large it yesterday.

The head noun of "picture" noun objects of verbs like *destroy* and *attack* also cannot be in the form of a definite pronoun:

(iv) a. *Oscar destroyed it about manatees.
    b. *Olga attacked it about extraction constraints..

The sentences in (iv) contrast with parallel sentences with verbs like *write* and *paint*:

(v) a. Oscar wrote it about manatees.
   b. Olga painted it of Millard Fillmore.

The sentences in (v) are clearly much more acceptable than those in (iv). This contrast is explained by the SAH. The verb *write* allows the structure in which the NP object and the PP are separate constituents under the VP. Thus, the pronoun is simply functioning as the NP, not a head noun. The verbs *destroy* and *attack*, on the other hand, allow only one structure. In (iv) the PP-attached-to-VP structure is not available; the PP can only be *within* the NP.

The third argument involves quantifier scope. Horn notes that quantifiers in "picture" nouns like the following are ambiguous:

(vi) Oscar wrote his first five books about Millard Fillmore in 1988.

On one reading the scope of the quantifier contains *books*, and on the other reading it contains *books about Millard Fillmore*. Thus, on the first reading it just happens that the first five books Oscar ever wrote were about Millard Fillmore, whereas on the second reading we are just talking about the first five books about Millard Fillmore that Oscar wrote (which could in fact have been his twelfth through sixteenth books).

When a quantifier such as *five* occurs in a corresponding sentence with *destroy*, it is unambiguous:

(vii) Oscar destroyed his first five books about Millard Fillmore.

Here the scope of the quantifier must be *books about Millard Fillmore*.

Horn claims that the ambiguity of (vi) results from the SAH. If the scope of the quantifier is the entire NP in which it is contained, then the two structures in (18) and (19) provide the correct scope distinction. The structure in (18) corresponds to the 'five books about Millard Fillmore' reading, and the structure in (19) corresponds to the 'five books' reading. The sentence in (vii) is not structurally ambiguous; it has only the structure in (18). Therefore, the quantifier in (vii) has only the 'five books about Millard Fillmore' reading.

Unfortunately, Horn's tests for structural ambiguity do not match perfectly with all the possible extraction cases. (Some of the problems with Horn's analysis are also noted in Bach and Horn 1976, Rodman 1977, and Erteschik-Shir 1981). Whereas in the case of verbs of creation such as *write* and *paint* the correlation holds between extraction and the other supposed indicators of structural ambiguity, for other extraction-permitting verbs the correlation fails. Extraction is allowed from objects of *see, read*, and *play*, but the results of the passivization and pronominalization tests are less acceptable:

(viii) a. Oscar read a book about manatees.
        b. What did Oscar read a book about?
        c. A book about manatees was read by Oscar.
        d. *A book was read about manatees by Oscar.
        e. *Oscar read it about manatees.

(ix)   a. Olga saw a painting of Otto Jespersen.
        b. Who did Olga see a painting of?
        c. A painting of Otto Jespersen was seen by Olga.
        d. *A painting was seen of Otto Jespersen by Olga.
        e. *Olga saw it of Otto Jespersen.

(x)   a. Otto played a sonata by Mozart.
        b. Who did Otto play a sonata by?
        c. A sonata by Mozart was played by Otto.
        d. *A sonata was played by Mozart by Otto.
        e. *Otto played it by Mozart.

The scope test also fails to accurately predict which verbs will permit extraction. Whereas extraction-permitting verbs such as *paint* and *write* do produce ambiguity with quantifiers, a number of extraction-permitting verbs do not:

(xi)   a. Oscar read his first five books about Millard Fillmore in 1988.
        b. Olga learned her first five poems by Goethe in 1988.
        c. Otto played his first five sonatas by Mozart in 1988.
        d. Oscar recited his first five sonnets by Petrarch.
        e. Olga saw her first five paintings of Hildegard von Bingen.
        f. Otto heard his first five operas by Wagner.

(xii)   a. Who did Oscar read a book about?
        b. Who did Olga learn a poem by?
        c. Who did Otto play a sonata by?
        d. Who did Oscar recite a sonnet by?
        e. Who did Olga see a painting of?
        f. Who did Otto hear an opera by?

Although all the verbs in (xi) permit extraction (as shown by (xii)), the sentences are all unambiguous, with the quantifier taking the wider scope (*five books about Millard Fillmore, five poems by Goethe*, etc.). The narrower scope reading is either very weak (as in the case of *read* in (xia)) or nonexistent. Once again, there is a mismatch between Horn's test and the property of permitting extraction.

Thus, Horn's tests plus extractability classify verbs into *three* groups roughly as shown in (xiii).

(xiii) *Verb classes and properties*

	Verb type		
	Creation	Using	Destruction
Horn's tests	yes	no	no
Extractability	yes	yes	no

10. In discussing these cases, Erteschik-Shir relies on what she calls "dominance tests" to show that in the cases where extraction is less good the NP involved is in fact presuppositional (a sentence element is dominant if it is not presupposed). The examples in (i) and (ii) illustrate this contrast with the two sentences in (23).

(i) Bill said, "John saw a picture of the present king of France."
     It's a lie—there is no King of France.

(ii) Bill said, "John destroyed a picture of the present king of France."
     *It's a lie—there is no king of France.

The principle behind the test shown in (i) and (ii) is that when existence is merely asserted rather than presupposed, the assertion can be refuted. Thus, the response to Bill's statement in (i) is an appropriate continuation. However, if existence is presupposed, a refutation is claimed to be inappropriate, and this is what is seen in (ii) (the judgment is Erteschik-Shir's). In (ii) not only is the existence of the picture presupposed, but the existence of the subject of the picture is presupposed as well.

   Although I agree with Erteschik-Shir's judgments regarding extraction in (23)–(24), it is not clear to me that the "dominance test" in (ii) genuinely sheds light on the issue of determining the factors that influence the acceptability of extraction from NP, nor do I agree with her judgment that there is a contrast between the continuations in (i) and (ii).

11. There is some evidence that scrambling may not be a unitary phenomenon in the Germanic languages—that it may involve not only adjunction to IP, but also a more local rule of object shift (see Holmberg 1986 and Webelhuth 1989). I examine only the cases that are clearly of the IP-adjunction type.

12. Just as in the case of diagnosing the position of subjects in German that I discussed in chapter 2, the sentential adverb actually acts as only a partial diagnostic. Although elements to the left of the adverb are unambiguously VP-external, elements to the right of the adverb can receive a VP-external interpretation under special intonational circumstances. Although there is clearly a relationship between focus and the presence or absence of presupposition accommodation, a comprehensive discussion of these facts is beyond the scope of this monograph. See Partee, to appear, and Krifka, to appear, for some discussion of the relationship between focus and the derivation of tripartite logical representations. In the discussion that follows I will assume the most neutral intonation, and regard the elements to the right of the adverbs as VP-internal.

13. Scrambling seems to have a similar semantic result in a number of other languages including Dutch (Kerstens 1975, De Haan 1979, Verhagen 1986) and

Hindi (Mahajan 1990). In Japanese, however, S-structure scrambling does not seem to have this semantic effect (Saito 1989, Tateishi 1991).

14. Moltmann (1991) gives an account of the semantic effects of scrambling that seems to require that all quantificational NPs scramble out of the VP. Her analysis is based on Safir's (1985) case-marking account of the so-called definiteness effect in *there*-insertion sentences, in which indefinite subject NPs can receive case within VP but definite subject NPs cannot. Moltmann extends this approach to all NPs, requiring definite, or quantificational, NPs to move out of VP to receive case. It is not clear to me how this rather strong claim (that all quantificational NPs must move out of VP at S-structure) can be justified, since there are many cases of strong object NPs in an apparently VP-internal position.

15. Another way of approaching this problem would be to use a form of Pesetsky's (1989) Earliness Principle, which states that certain conditions have to be satisfied "as early as possible" in the derivation (the Earliness Principle is a variation on the Principle of Economy formulated by Chomsky (1991)). In this case, variable binding by an operator would have to be achieved as early as possible in the derivation. German, allowing scrambling, could satisfy this constraint with respect to quantificational NPs at S-structure. Since English has no S-structure scrambling rule, QR must take place at the later level of LF. One problem with this approach is that it does not explain the optionality of scrambling in German. It is not true that the condition on variable binding *must* be satisfied at S-structure in German, merely that it *can* be satisfied at an earlier level than in English.

16. The relevance of "repeatability" of action to the possibility of variable binding is also noted in De Hoop and De Swart 1990 and De Swart 1991.

17. I have taken care to limit myself to those experiencer predicates that permit *only* an individual-level interpretation, avoiding verbs such as *enjoy*, which seem to also permit a stage-level interpretation roughly paraphrasable as 'to partake of with pleasure'.

18. A couple of my informants find (53a) and (53b) to be slightly better than the rest, but still within the "unacceptable" range of the grammaticality scale.

19. In the extraction examples in (55b) and (56b) (which involve fronting of the inflected verb due to the verb-second constraint) I use the compound past rather than the simple past that would be parallel to the unextracted cases in order to make the relative positions of the object NPs clearer.

20. It should be noted that there is a construction in German that involves "long-distance scrambling" (i.e., non-clause-bound scrambling) in which object NPs can scramble out of infinitival complements of a limited class of control verbs. This construction has also been called the "third construction" (see Den Besten et al. 1988, Den Besten and Rutten 1989, and Bayer and Kornfilt 1991). Interestingly, this construction does not exhibit the constraint on extraction shown in (56) and (58) (example from Bayer and Kornfilt):

(i) Was$_i$ hat Hilda [t$_i$ für einem Kind]$_j$ vergessen [PRO t$_j$ die Zebras zu zeigen]?
     what has Hilda   for a   child   forgotten   the zebras to show
     'What kind of child has Hilda forgotten to show the zebras?'

I will not deal with the properties of this construction here, but will simply regard it as being substantively different from the cases of clause-bound scrambling that I am considering.

21. The sentence is grammatical on a reading where the verb *schätzen* 'appreciate' is given a meaning similar to that of *enjoy* in a sentence such as *Every morning I sit and enjoy a cup of tea*. In this context the verb has a meaning closer to 'consume—or in the case of operas, listen to—with pleasure', and may thus fall into another category of verb, closer to that of *read* in its semantic properties.

22. A number of questions remain. For example, this account does not explain the fact that generic indefinite subjects also can freely appear in the weak crossover configuration, as noted by Postal (1970) and Wasow (1979):

(i) If he$_i$ has an unruly herd of sheep, a farmer$_i$ should acquire a border collie.

This is also left unexplained by Fodor and Sag's analysis of specific indefinites, however.

23. There is another class of verbs that is somewhat problematic. These are the verbs like *type* and *copyedit*. As observed by Erteschik-Shir (1973), these verbs are also somewhat resistant to extraction from their object NPs.

(i) a. *?Who did you copyedit a book by?
    b. *?What did you type a book about?
    c. ?What did you print an article about?
    d. *?What did you revise a novel about?

Here again the problematic examples are given in an episodic tense. The judgments in (i) hold for very neutral contexts, but in a context where typing and copyediting activities are habitual, such as in a generic sentence with *usually*, the extraction improves (although *revise* is for presumably pragmatic reasons resistant to a generic interpretation).

(ii) a. Who do you usually copyedit books by?
    b. What do you usually type books about?
    c. What do you usually print articles about?
    d. ??What do you usually revise novels about?

A habitual reading can also be brought about by a context in which the primary goal of the action is to create a *typed* or *copyedited* manuscript. For example, if the subject of the sentence is a secretary, an editor, or some other relevant professional agent, extraction is also less bad than in the neutral contexts in (i):

(iii) a. What did the secretary type a book about?
    b. Who did the editor copyedit an article by?
    c. What did the *Hampshire Gazette* print an article about?
    d. ?What did the ghostwriter rewrite a book about?

In (iii) the preexistence of the books and articles is not relevant because the focus is on the production of typed, copyedited, printed, and rewritten versions, none of which are preexisting.

24. This classification of verbs suggests that there should be some degrading of grammaticality in generic contexts if a verb that selects the quantificational reading

is conjoined with a verb that selects the existential reading. This does seem to be the case:

(i) a. ?Hector always bakes and hates cakes.
   b. ?Horace always writes and despises novels.
   c. Hector always bakes and serves cakes.
   d. Horace always writes and reads novels.

The contrast is subtle, but there does seem to be a difference between an existential-selecting verb conjoined with an experiencer verb (which does not allow the existential reading) and the same verb conjoined with a verb of using (which does allow the existential reading).

25. The constraint in (85) has the appearance of a constraint on representations rather than on movement, but Chomsky actually remains uncommitted on this issue (Chomsky 1986a: 93, n. 25).

26. Bayer and Kornfilt (1991) attribute the ungrammaticality in the scrambled case to a violation of the Principle of Unambiguous Binding of Müller and Sternefeld (1990):

(i) *Principle of Unambiguous Binding*
   A variable cannot be simultaneously bound by an operator position and a
   scrambling position.

A closer examination of the structure involved reveals that this cannot be the case, since the *wh*-phrase and the scrambled NP bind distinct (i.e., noncoindexed) traces:

(ii) *Was$_i$ hat [$_{IP}$ Otto [$_{IP}$[$_{NP}$ t$_i$ für Romane]$_j$ immer t$_j$ gelesen]]?
     what has   Otto   for novels   always read

Thus, there is no "simultaneous binding" taking place here. I do not rule out the possibility that the ungrammaticality might result from some sort of "improper movement" from a scrambling position to the [Spec, CP] position (see Müller and Sternefeld 1990), but since the typology of scrambling positions is far from clear (the literature is quite inconclusive), I will leave this possibility for further research.

27. Browning notes that an adjoined segment must be prevented from *triggering* inheritance in another category if adjunction is to be able to provide "escape hatches," such as in the case of adjoining to VP in order to void the barrierhood of VP. It is not clear that adjunction to VP is actually necessary in these cases (see, for example, the discussion in Müller and Sternefeld 1990), so I will remain neutral on the issue of whether adjoined segments can trigger barrierhood of a segment of another category.

28. Proposing that Subjacency can apply at LF runs directly counter to proposals such as that of Lasnik and Saito (1984) in which intermediate traces may delete at LF, since if these traces deleted, they would yield Subjacency violations. One way around this would be to have the LF constraint apply only to those links of the chain created by LF movement operations.

29. Additional evidence for the necessity of an order-independent constraint that constrains LF *wh*-movement as well comes from Japanese. As pointed out to me by Koichi Tateishi, in Japanese the quantificational reading of an indefinite object is ruled out in extraction environments even though *both* QR and *wh*-movement

occur at LF. In a generic declarative sentence both the existential and quantificational readings of the object are possible:

(i) Jon-wa kanarazu   Chomusukii-no hon-o   yomu.
    John   without-fail Chomsky-GEN book-ACC read
    'John always reads Chomsky's books.'

In a question, only the existential reading is possible:

(ii) Jon-wa kanarazu   dare-no hon-o yomu-ka-ne?
     John   without-fail who   book read-Q
     'Who does John always read a book by?'

Thus, the necessary constraint cannot be a constraint on S-structure movement of a *wh*-phrase.

30. This raises the question of whether other island effects (such as *wh*-islands) could also be explained in terms of a syntactic operation of presupposition accommodation. Recent work by Comorovski (1989) and Berman (1991) suggests that they might be. I leave the explanation of *wh*-islands and other island effects as a matter for future research.

31. As pointed out to me by David Pesetsky, it is possible to state the needed restriction as a constraint on movement rather than representations. If positions are characterized as being either "blocking" or "nonblocking," the desired result could be attained by a filter prohibiting nonblocking categories (e.g. L-marked categories) from moving to a blocking position:

(i) *[−blocking] in a [+blocking] position.

At first blush, it appears that the movement filter approach is empirically equivalent to the constraint on traces approach. There is one situation that could distinguish the two, however. If an L-marked category could move to a [+blocking] position, and then move back to its original [−blocking] position (by some kind of yo-yo-like movement process), it would violate the filter in (i), but not necessarily a representational subjacency constraint. I do not know of any language with the necessary sort of construction for making the distinction, however. Therefore, I will stick with the simpler representational approach.

32. Guéron (1981) explains the facts in (100) by means of her Complete Constituent Constraint (p. 86), which states that a complete constituent (a constituent governed by a logical operator) cannot contain a free variable.

References

Abney, S. (1987). "The Noun Phrase in Its Sentential Aspect." Ph.D. dissertation, MIT.

Babby, L. (1980). *Existential Sentences and Negation in Russian*. Ann Arbor, Mich.: Karoma Publishers.

Bach, E. (1968). "Nouns and Noun Phrases." In E. Bach and R. T. Harms (eds.). *Universals in Linguistic Theory*, 91–122. New York: Holt, Rinehart and Winston.

Bach, E., and G. Horn (1976). "Remarks on 'Conditions on Transformations'." *Linguistic Inquiry* 7, 265–299.

Bacon, J. (1965). "A Simple Treatment of Complex Terms." *Journal of Philosophy* 62, 328–331.

Baltin, M. (1981). "Strict Bounding." In C. L. Baker and J. McCarthy (eds.). *The Logical Problem of Language Acquisition*, 257–295. Cambridge, Mass.: MIT Press.

Baltin, M. (1984). "Extraposition Rules and Discontinuous Constituents." *Linguistic Inquiry* 15, 155–162.

Baltin, M. (1987). "Do Antecedent-Contained Deletions Exist?" *Linguistic Inquiry* 18, 579–595.

Barss, A. (1986). 'Chains and Anaphoric Dependencies." Ph.D. dissertation, MIT.

Barwise, J., and R. Cooper (1981). "Generalized Quantifiers and Natural Language." *Linguistics and Philosophy* 4, 159–219.

Bayer, J., and J. Kornfilt (1991). "Against Scrambling as Move-Alpha." In *Proceedings of NELS 21*, 1–15. GLSA, University of Massachusetts, Amherst.

Belletti, A. (1988). "The Case of Unaccusatives." *Linguistic Inquiry* 19, 1–34.

Belletti, A., and L. Rizzi (1988). "Psych Verbs and θ-Theory." *Natural Language and Linguistic Theory* 6, 291–352.

Belnap, N. (1970). "Conditional Assertion and Restricted Quantification. *Noûs* 4, 1–12.

Bennis, H. (1983). "A Case of Restructuring." In H. Bennis and W. U. S. van Lessen Kloeke (eds.) *Linguistics in the Netherlands 1983*, 9–19. Dordrecht: Foris.

Bennis, H. (1986). *Gaps and Dummies*. Dordrecht: Foris.

Berman, S. (1991). "On the Semantics and Logical Form of WH-Clauses." Ph.D. dissertation, University of Massachusetts, Amherst.

Besten, H. den (1985). "The Ergative Hypothesis and Free Word Order in Dutch and German." In J. Toman (ed.) *Studies on German Grammar*, 23–64. Dordrecht: Foris.

Besten, H. den, and J. Rutten (1989). "On Verb Raising, Extraposition, and Free Word Order in Dutch." In D. Jaspers, W. Klooster, Y. Putseys, and P. Seuren (eds.) *Sentential Complementation and the Lexicon: Studies in Honor of Wim de Geest*, 41–56. Dordrecht: Foris.

Besten, H. den, J. Rutten, T. Veenstra, and J. Veld (1988). "Verb raising, extrapositie en de derde constructie." Ms., Universiteit van Amsterdam.

Bhatt, C. (1990). *Die syntaktische Struktur der Nominalphrase im Deutschen*. Tübingen: Gunter Narr Verlag.

Bonet, E. (1989). "Postverbal Subjects in Catalan." Ms., MIT.

Bouton, L. (1970). "Antecedent-Contained Pro-Forms." In *Papers from the Sixth Regional Meeting, Chicago Linguistic Society*, 154–167. Chicago Linguistic Society, University of Chicago.

Bowers, J. (1988). "Extended X-Bar Theory, the ECP, and the Left Branch Condition." In *Proceedings of the West Coast Conference on Formal Linguistics* 7, 47–62. Stanford Linguistics Association, Stanford University.

Brame, M. (1981). "The General Theory of Binding and Fusion." *Linguistic Analysis* 7, 277–325.

Bresnan, J. (1973). "Syntax of the Comparative Clause Construction in English." *Linguistic Inquiry* 4, 275–344.

Browning, M. A. (1991). "Bounding Conditions on Representation." *Linguistic Inquiry* 22, 541–562.

Carlson, A. (1978). "A Diachronic Treatment of English Quantifiers." *Lingua* 46, 295–328.

Carlson, G. (1977a). "Amount Relatives." *Language* 53, 520–542.

Carlson, G. (1977b). "Reference to Kinds in English." Ph.D. dissertation, University of Massachusetts, Amherst.

Carlson, G. (1989). "On the Semantic Composition of English Generic Sentences." In G. Chierchia, B. H. Partee, and R. Turner (eds.). *Properties. Types, and Meaning. Volume 2: Semantic Issues*, 167–192. Dordrecht: Kluwer.

Chomsky, N. (1971). "Deep Structure, Surface Structure, and Semantic Interpretation." In D. Steinberg and L. Jakobovits (eds.). *Semantics: An Interdisciplinary*

Reader in Philosophy, Linguistics, and Psychology, 183–216. Cambridge: Cambridge University Press.

Chomsky, N. (1973). "Conditions on Transformations." In S. R. Anderson and P. Kiparsky (eds.) *A Festschrift for Morris Halle*, 232–286. New York: Holt, Rinehart and Winston. [Reprinted in *Essays on Form and Interpretation*. New York: North-Holland. 1977.]

Chomsky, N. (1975). "Questions of Form and Interpretation." *Linguistic Analysis* 1, 75–109.

Chomsky, N. (1976). "Conditions on Rules of Grammar." *Linguistic Analysis* 2, 303–352. [Reprinted in *Essays on Form and Interpretation*. New York: North-Holland. 1977.]

Chomsky, N. (1977). "On Wh-Movement." In P. Culicover, T. Wasow, and A. Akmajian (eds.) *Formal Syntax*, 71–155. New York: Academic Press.

Chomsky, N. (1981). *Lectures on Government and Binding*. Dordrecht: Foris.

Chomsky, N. (1986a). *Barriers*. Cambridge, Mass.: MIT Press.

Chomsky, N. (1986b). *Knowledge of Language*. New York: Praeger.

Chomsky, N. (1991). "Some Notes on Economy of Derivation and Representation." In R. Freidin (ed.) *Principles and Parameters in Comparative Grammar*, 417–454. Cambridge, Mass.: MIT Press.

Comorovski, I. (1989). "Discourse and the Syntax of Multiple Constituent Questions." Ph.D. dissertation, Cornell University.

Cooper, R. (1979). "The Interpretation of Pronouns." In F. Heny and H. Schnelle (eds.). *Syntax and Semantics 10: Selections from the Third Groningen Roundtable*, 61–92. New York: Academic Press.

Daneš, F. (1960). "Sentence Intonation from a Functional Point of View." *Word* 16, 34–54.

Daneš, F. (1964). "A Three-Level Approach to Syntax." *Travaux Linguistiques de Prague* 1, 225–240.

Davidson, D. (1967). "The Logical Form of Action Sentences." In N. Rescher (ed.). *The Logic of Decision and Action*, 81–95. Pittsburgh, Pa: University of Pittsburgh Press.

DeCarrico, J. (1983). "On Quantifier Raising." *Linguistic Inquiry* 14, 343–346.

Déprez, V. (1989). "On the Typology of Syntactic Positions and the Nature of Chains: Move α to the Specifier of Functional Projections." Ph.D. dissertation, MIT.

Diesing, M. (1988). "Bare Plurals and the Stage/Individual Contrast." In M. Krifka (ed.). *Genericity in Natural Language: Proceedings of the 1988 Tübingen Conference*, 107–154. SNS-Bericht 88-42, Seminar für natürlich-sprachliche Systeme, Universität Tübingen.

Diesing, M. (1990a). "Verb-Second in Yiddish and the Nature of the Subject Position." *Natural Language and Linguistic Theory* 8, 41–79.

Diesing, M. (1990b). "The Syntactic Roots of Semantic Partition." Ph.D. dissertation, University of Massachusetts, Amherst.

Donnellan, K. (1966). "Reference and Definite Descriptions." *Philosophical Review* 75, 281–304.

É. Kiss, K. (1987). *Configurationality in Hungarian.* Dordrecht: Reidel.

Enç, M. (1991). "The Semantics of Specificity." *Linguistic Inquiry* 22, 1–25.

Erguvanli, E. (1984). *The Function of Word Order in Turkish Grammar.* University of California Publications in Linguistics vol. 106. Berkeley and Los Angeles: University of California Press.

Erteschik-Shir, N. (1973). "On the Nature of Island Constraints." Ph.D. dissertation, MIT. [Distributed by the Indiana University Linguistics Club, 1977.]

Erteschik-Shir, N. (1981). "On Extraction from Noun Phrases (Picture Noun Phrases)." In A. Belletti, L. Brandi, and L. Rizzi (eds.). *Theory of Markedness in Generative Grammar: Proceedings of the 1979 GLOW Conference,* 147–169. Pisa: Scuola Normale Superiore di Pisa.

Evans, G. (1977). "Pronouns, Quantifiers, and Relative Clauses." *Canadian Journal of Philosophy* 7, 467–536.

Fanselow, G. (1986). "Scrambling and Barriers." Ms., Universität Passau, read at the GGS-Conference at Regensburg 1989.

Fanselow, G. (1987). *Konfigurationalität.* Tübingen: Gunter Narr Verlag.

Fanselow, G. (1988a). "Aufspaltung von NPn und das Problem der 'freien' Wortstellung." *Linguistische Berichte* 114, 91–112.

Fanselow, G. (1988b). "German Word Order and Universal Grammar." In U. Reyle and C. Rohrer (eds.). *Natural Language Parsing and Linguistic Theories,* 317–355. Dordrecht: Reidel.

Farkas, D., and Y. Sugioka (1983). "Restrictive If/When Clauses." *Linguistics and Philosophy* 9, 225–258.

Fiengo, R., and J. Higginbotham (1981). "Opacity in NP." *Linguistic Analysis* 7, 395–422.

Firbas, J. (1970). "On the Interplay of Means of Functional Sentence Perspective." In *Actes du Xe Congrès International des Linguistes,* Vol. 2, 741–745. Bucharest: Editura Academiei Republicii Socialiste Romania.

Fodor, J. D., and I. Sag (1982). "Referential and Quantificational Indefinites." *Linguistics and Philosophy* 5, 355–398.

Freidin, R. (1978). "Cyclicity and the Theory of Grammar." *Linguistic Inquiry* 9, 19–49.

Fukui, N. (1986). "A Theory of Category Projection and Its Applications." Ph.D. dissertation, MIT.

Fukui, N., and M. Speas (1986). "Specifiers and Projection." In *MIT Working Papers in Linguistics* 8, 128–172. Department of Linguistics and Philosophy, MIT.

Gerstner, C., and M. Krifka (1987). "Genericity." Ms., Universität Tübingen.

Giusti, G. (1990). "Floating Quantifiers, Scrambling, and Configurationality." *Linguistic Inquiry* 21, 633–641.

Grice, H. P. (1975). "Logic and Conversation." In P. Cole and J. L. Morgan (eds.). *Syntax and Semantics 3*, 41–58. New York: Academic Press.

Gruber, J. (1965). "Studies in Lexical Relations." Ph.D dissertation, MIT.

Guéron, J. (1980). "The Syntax and Semantics of PP Extraposition." *Linguistic Inquiry* 11, 637–678.

Guéron, J. (1981). "Logical Operators, Complete Constituents, and Extraction Transformations." In R. May and J. Koster (eds.). *Levels of Syntactic Representation*, 65–142. Dordrecht: Foris.

Guéron, J., and R. May (1984). "Extraposition and Logical Form." *Linguistic Inquiry* 15, 1–31.

Gussenhoven, C. (1984). *On the Grammar and Semantics of Sentence Accents.* Dordrecht: Foris.

Haan, G. de (1979). *Conditions on Rules: The Proper Balance between Syntax and Semantics.* Dordrecht: Foris.

Haegeman, L. (1991). *Introduction to Government and Binding Theory.* Oxford: Blackwell.

Haider, H. (1983). "Connectedness Effects in German." In *Groningen Arbeiten zur Germanistischen Linguistik* 23, 82–119. Rijksuniversiteit Groningen.

Hailperin, T. (1957). "A Theory of Restricted Quantification." *Journal of Symbolic Logic* 22, 19–35, 113–129.

Hasegawa, H. (1988). "On Antecedent-Contained Deletion." *English Linguistics* 5, 191–196.

Hausser, R. (1973). "Presuppositions and quantifiers." In *Papers from the Ninth Regional Meeting, Chicago Linguistic Society*, 192–204. Chicago Linguistic Society, University of Chicago.

Heim, I. (1982). "The Semantics of Definite and Indefinite Noun Phrases." Ph.D. dissertation, University of Massachusetts, Amherst.

Heim, I. (1983). "On the Projection Problem for Presuppositions." In *Proceedings of the West Coast Conference on Formal Linguistics* 2, 114–125. Stanford Linguistics Association, Stanford University.

Heim, I. (1990). "E-Type Pronouns and Donkey Anaphora." *Linguistics and Philosophy* 13, 137–177.

Hellan, L. (1986). "The Headedness of NPs in Norwegian." In P. Muysken and H. van Riemsdijk (eds.). *Features and Projections*, 89–122. Dordrecht: Foris.

Hentschel, E. (1986). *Funktion und Geschichte deutscher Partikeln: Ja, doch, halt und eben.* Tübingen: Max Niemeyer Verlag.

Hestvik, A. (1990). "LF-Movement of Pronouns and the Computation of Binding Domains." Ph.D. dissertation, Brandeis University.

Higginbotham, J. (1985). "On Semantics." *Linguistic Inquiry* 16, 547–593.

Higginbotham, J. (1987). "Indefiniteness and Predication." In E. Reuland and A. ter Meulen (eds.) *The Representation of (In)definiteness*, 43–70. Cambridge, Mass.: MIT Press.

Higginbotham, J. (1989). "Elucidations of Meaning." *Linguistics and Philosophy* 12, 463–517.

Hirschbuhler, P. (1982). "VP-Deletion and Across-the-Board Quantifier Scope." In *Proceedings of NELS 12*, 132–139. GLSA, University of Massachusetts, Amherst.

Holmberg, A. (1986). "Word Order and Syntactic Features in the Scandinavian Languages." Ph.D. dissertation, Universitet Stockholms.

Hoop, H. de (1990). "Existential Sentences in Dutch and English." To appear in *First LCJL Proceedings*. Rijksuniversiteit Groningen.

Hoop, H. de, and M. Kas (1989). "Sommige betekenisaspecten van enkele kwantoren, oftewel: enkele betekenisaspecten van sommige kwantoren." Ms., Rijksuniversiteit Groningen.

Hoop, H. de, and H. de Swart (1990). "Indefinite Objects." In R. Bok-Bennema and P. Coopmans (eds.). *Linguistics in the Netherlands 1990*, 91–100. Dordrecht: Foris.

Horn, G. M. (1974). "The Noun Phrase Constraint." Ph.D. dissertation, University of Massachusetts, Amherst.

Horn, L. (1972). "On the Semantic Properties of Logical Operators in English." Ph.D. dissertation, University of California at Los Angeles. [Distributed by the Indiana University Linguistics Club, 1976.]

Hornstein, N. (1984). *Logic as Grammar*. Cambridge, Mass.: MIT Press.

Huang, C.-T. J. (1982). "Logical Relations in Chinese and the Theory of Grammar." Ph.D. dissertation, MIT.

Hudson, W. (1989). "Functional Categories and the Saturation of Noun Phrases," In *Proceedings of NELS 19*, 207–222. GLSA, University of Massachusetts, Amherst.

Ioup, G. (1975). "The Treatment of Quantifier Scope in a Transformational Grammar." Ph.D. dissertation, CUNY Graduate Center.

Jackendoff, R. S. (1968). "Quantifiers in English." *Foundations of Language* 4, 422–442.

Jackendoff, R. S. (1972). *Semantic Interpretation in Generative Grammar*. Cambridge, Mass.: MIT Press.

Jackendoff, R. S. (1977). $\bar{X}$ *Syntax: A Study of Phrase Structure*. Cambridge, Mass.: MIT Press.

Jacobs, J. (1984). "The Syntax of Focus and Adverbials in German." In W. Abraham and S. de Mey (eds.) *Topic, Focus, and Configurationality*, 101–127. Amsterdam: John Benjamins.

Jespersen, O. (1927). *A Modern English Grammar on Historical Principles*. Heidelberg: C. Winter.

Jong, F. de, and H. Verkuyl (1985). "Generalized Quantifiers: The Properness of Their Strength." In J. van Benthem and A. ter Meulen (eds.) *Generalized Quantifiers in Natural Language*. 21–43. Dordrecht: Foris.

Kadmon, N. (1987). "On Unique and Non-Unique Reference and Asymmetric Quantification." Ph.D. dissertation, University of Massachusetts, Amherst.

Kamp, J. A. W. (1981). "A Theory of Truth and Semantic Representation." In J. Groenendijk, T. Janssen, and M. Stokhof (eds.) *Formal Methods in the Study of Language*, 277–321. Amsterdam: Mathematical Centre.

Kathol, A. (1989). "Adverbial Quantification and Scrambled Objects." In *Papers on Quantification*. NSF Grant Report, Department of Linguistics, University of Massachusetts, Amherst.

Kayne, R. (1981). "ECP Extensions." *Linguistic Inquiry* 12, 93–133.

Kayne, R. (1984). *Connectedness and Binary Branching*. Dordrecht: Foris.

Kerstens, J. (1975). "Ofer afgeliede struktuur en de interpretatie van zinnen." Ms., Universiteit van Amsterdam.

Kitagawa, Y. (1986). "Subject in Japanese and English." Ph.D. dissertation, University of Massachusetts, Amherst.

Koopman, H., and D. Sportiche (1982). "Variables and the Bijection Principle." *The Linguistic Review* 2, 139–160.

Koopman, H., and D. Sportiche (1985). "Theta Theory and Extraction." *GLOW Newsletter* 14, 57–58.

Koopman, H., and D. Sportiche (1988). "Subjects." Ms., University of California at Los Angeles.

Koster, J. (1978). *Locality Principles in Syntax*. Dordrecht: Foris.

Koster, J. (1987). *Domains and Dynasties: The Radical Autonomy of Syntax*. Dordrecht: Foris.

Kratzer, A. (1978). *Semantik der Rede*. Königstein: Scriptor.

Kratzer, A. (1981). "The Notional Category of Modality." In H. Eikmeyer and H. Rieser (eds.). *Words, Worlds and Contexts: New Approaches in Word Semantics.* Berlin: de Gruyter.

Kratzer, A. (1986). "Conditionals." In A. M. Farley, P. Farley, and K. E. McCullough (eds.). *Papers from the Parasession on Pragmatics and Grammatical Theory*, 1–15. Chicago Linguistic Society, University of Chicago.

Kratzer, A. (1989). "Stage and Individual Level Predicates." In *Papers on Quantification.* NSF Grant Report, Department of Linguistics, University of Massachusetts, Amherst.

Krifka, M. (1988). "The Relational Theory of Genericity." In M. Krifka (ed.). *Genericity in Natural Language: Proceedings of the 1988 Tübingen Conference*, 285–312. SNS-Bericht 88–42, Seminar für natürlich-sprachliche Systeme, Universität Tübingen.

Krifka, M. (to appear). "Focus and Genericity." In G. Carlson and F. J. Pelletier (eds.) *The Generic Book.* Chicago: University of Chicago Press.

Krifka, M., and C. Gerstner (1987). "An Outline of Genericity." SNS-Bericht 87–25, Seminar für natürlich-sprachliche Systeme, Universität Tübingen.

Kripke, S. (1977). "Speaker's Reference and Semantic Reference." In P. French, T. Uehling, and H. Wettstein (eds.) *Contemporary Perspectives in the Philosophy of Language*, 6–27. Minneapolis, Minn.: University of Minnesota Press.

Kroch, A. (1974). "The Semantics of Scope in English." Ph.D. dissertation, MIT.

Kuroda, S.-Y. (1988). "Whether We Agree or Not: A Comparative Syntax of English and Japanese." *Lingvisticae Investigationes* 12, 1–47.

Lappin, S., and T. Reinhart (1988). "Presuppositional Effects of Strong Determiners: A Processing Account." *Linguistics* 26, 1021–1037.

Larson, R. (1988). "On the Double Object Construction." *Linguistic Inquiry* 19, 335–392.

Larson, R., and R. May (1990). "Antecedent Containment or Vacuous Movement: A Reply to Baltin." *Linguistic Inquiry* 21, 103–122.

Lasnik, H., and M. Saito (1984). "On the Nature of Proper Government." *Linguistic Inquiry* 15, 235–289.

Lasnik, H., and M. Saito (1992). *Move α.* Cambridge, Mass.: MIT Press.

Lenerz, J. (1977). *Zur Abfolge nominaler Satzglieder im Deutschen.* Tübingen: Gunter Narr Verlag.

Lewis, D. (1975). "Adverbs of Quantification." In E. Keenan (ed.) *Formal Semantics of Natural Language*, 3–15. Cambridge: Cambridge University Press.

Lewis, D. (1979). "Scorekeeping in a Language Game." In R. Bäuerle, U. Egli, and A. von Stechow (eds.). *Semantics from Different Points of View*, 172–187. Berlin: Springer.

References 165

Lötscher, A. (1983). *Satzakzent und Funktionale Satzperspektive im Deutschen.* Tübingen: Max Niemeyer Verlag.

Ludlow, P., and S. Neale (1991). "Indefinite Descriptions: In Defense of Russell." *Linguistics and Philosophy* 14, 171–202.

McCawley, J. (1988). *The Syntactic Phenomena of English.* Chicago: University of Chicago Press.

McDaniel, D. (1989). "Partial and Multiple Wh-Movement." *Natural Language and Linguistic Theory* 7, 565–604.

Mahajan, A. (1990). "The A/A-bar Distinction and Movement Theory." Ph.D. dissertation, MIT.

May, R. (1977). "The Grammar of Quantification." Ph.D. dissertation, MIT.

May, R. (1985). *Logical Form: Its Structure and Derivation.* Cambridge, Mass.: MIT Press.

May, R. (1988). "Ambiguities of Quantification and *Wh*: A Reply to Williams." *Linguistic Inquiry* 19, 118–135.

May, R. (1989). "Interpreting Logical Form." *Linguistics and Philosophy* 12, 387–435.

Mey, S. de (1980). "Stages and Extensionality: The Carlson Problem." In S. Daalder and M. Gerritsen (eds.) *Linguistics in the Netherlands 1980,* 191–202. Dordrecht: Foris.

Milsark, G. (1974). "Existential Sentences in English." Ph.D. dissertation, MIT.

Moltmann, F. (1989). "Adjectives and Argument Structure in German." Ms., MIT.

Moltmann, F. (1991). "Scrambling in German and the Specificity Effect." Ms., MIT.

Müller, G., and W. Sternefeld (1990). "Improper Movement." Arbeitspapier Nr. 26, Fachgruppe Sprachwissenschaft der Universität Konstanz.

Neale, S. (1990). *Descriptions.* Cambridge, Mass: MIT Press.

Neidle, C. (1988). *The Role of Case in Russian Syntax.* Dordrecht: Kluwer.

Olsen, S. (1989). "AGR (eement). in the German Noun Phrase." in C. Bhatt, E. Löbel, and C. Schmidt (eds.) *Syntactic Phrase Structure Phenomena in Noun Phrases and Sentences,* 39–49. Amsterdam: John Benjamins.

Partee, B. H. (1972). "Opacity, Coreference, and Pronouns." In D. Davidson and G. Harman (eds.). *Semantics of Natural Language,* 415–441. Dordrecht: Reidel.

Partee, B. H. (1977). "John Is Easy to Please." In A. Zampolli (ed.) *Linguistic Structures Processing,* 281–312. Amsterdam: North-Holland.

Partee, B. H. (1978). "Bound Variables and Other Anaphors." In D. Waltz (ed.). *Proceedings of TINLAP 3.* The University of Illinois, Urbana.

Partee, B. H. (1988). "Many Quantifiers." In *Proceedings of ESCOL 1988*. Department of Linguistics, Ohio State University.

Partee, B. H. (to appear). "Topic, Focus, and Quantification." In *Proceedings of the 1991 SALT Conference*. Department of Modern Languages and Literatures, Cornell University.

Pesetsky, D. (1982). "Paths and Categories." Ph.D. dissertation, MIT.

Pesetsky, D. (1987). "Wh-in-Situ: Movement and Unselective Binding." In E. Reuland and A. ter Meulen (eds.) *The Representation of (In)definiteness*, 98–129. Cambridge, Mass.: MIT Press.

Pesetsky, D. (1989). "Language-Particular Processes and the Earliness Principle." Ms., MIT.

Pollock, J.-Y. (1989). "Verb Movement, Universal Grammar, and the Structure of IP." *Linguistic Inquiry* 20, 365–424.

Postal, P. (1970). "On Coreferential Complement Subject Deletion." *Linguistic Inquiry* 1, 439–500.

Reinhart, T. (1983). "Coreference and Bound Anaphora." *Linguistics and Philosophy* 6, 47–88.

Reinhart, T. (1987). "Specifier and Operator Binding." In E. Reuland and A. ter Meulen (eds.) *The Representation of (In)definiteness*, 130–167. Cambridge, Mass.: MIT Press.

Reuland, E. (1988). "Indefinite Subjects." In *Proceedings of NELS 18*, 375–394. GLSA, University of Massachusetts, Amherst.

Riemsdijk, H. van (1989). "Movement and Regeneration." In P. Benincà (ed.) *Linguistic Theory and Dialectology*. Dordrecht: Foris.

Rodman, R. (1977). "Concerning the NP Constraint." *Linguistic Inquiry* 8, 181–184.

Rooth, M. (1985). "Association with Focus." Ph.D. dissertation, University of Massachusetts, Amherst.

Rooth, M. (1991). "A Restrictive Theory of Focus Interpretation, or What Is the Source of Association with Focus Ambiguities?" Colloquium, University of Massachusetts, Amherst.

Ross, J. R. (1967). "Constraints on Variables in Syntax." Ph.D. dissertation, MIT.

Rothstein, S. (1988). "Conservativity and the Syntax of Determiners." *Linguistics* 26, 999–1019.

Rullmann, H. (1989). "Indefinite NPs in Dutch." In *Papers on Quantification*. NSF Grant Report, Department of Linguistics, University of Massachusetts, Amherst.

Russell, B. (1905). "On Denoting." *Mind* 14, 479–493.

Russell, B. (1919). *Introduction to Mathematical Philosophy*. London: Allen and Unwin.

Safir, K. (1983). "On Small Clauses as Constituents." *Linguistic Inquiry* 14, 730–735.

Safir, K. (1985). *Syntactic Chains*. Cambridge: Cambridge University Press.

Sag, I. (1976). "Deletion and Logical Form." Ph.D. dissertation, MIT.

Saito, M. (1989). "Scrambling as Semantically Vacuous A′-Movement." In M. Baltin and A. Kroch (eds.) *Alternative Conceptions of Phrase Structure*, 182–200. Chicago: University of Chicago Press.

Saito, M., and H. Hoji (1983). "Weak Crossover and Move Alpha in Japanese." *Natural Language and Linguistic Theory* 1, 245–259.

Schubert, L., and J. Pelletier (1989). "Generically Speaking, or Using Discourse Representation Theory to Interpret Generics." In G. Chierchia, B. H. Partee, and R. Turner (eds.) *Properties, Types, and Meaning. Volume 2: Semantic Issues*, 193–268, Dordrecht: Kluwer.

Selkirk, E. O. (1970). "On the Determiner Systems of Noun Phrase and Adjective Phrase." Ms., MIT.

Selkirk, E. O. (1977). "Some Remarks on Noun Phrase Structure." In P. Culicover, T. Wasow, and A. Akmajian (eds.). *Formal Syntax*, 285–316. New York: Academic Press.

Selkirk, E. O. (1984). *Phonology and Syntax: The Relation between Sound and Structure*. Cambridge, Mass: MIT Press.

Sigurðsson, H. (1990). "Icelandic Case-Marked PRO and the Licensing of Lexical A-Positions." In *Working Papers in Scandinavian Syntax* 45, 35–82. Department of Scandinavian Linguistics, Universitet Lund. [To appear in *Natural Language and Linguistic Theory*.]

Soames, S. (1989). "Presupposition." In D. M. Gabbay and F. Guenther (eds.). *Handbook of Philosophical Logic. Volume IV: Topics in the Philosophy of Language*, 553–616. Dordrecht: Reidel.

Speas, M. (1990). *Phrase Structure in Natural Language*. Dordrecht: Kluwer.

Sportiche, D. (1988). "A Theory of Floating Quantifiers and Its Corollaries for Constituent Structure." *Linguistic Inquiry* 19, 425–450.

Stechow, A. von (1990). "Current Issues in the theory of focus." Arbeitspapier Nr 24, Fachgruppe Sprachwissenschaft der Universität Konstanz.

Stechow, A. von, and W. Sternefeld (1988). *Bausteine syntaktischen Wissens: Ein Lehrbuch der generativen Grammatik*. Opladen: Westdeutscher Verlag.

Stowell, T. (1981). "Origins of Phrase Structure." Ph.D. dissertation, MIT.

Stowell, T. (1989). "Subjects, Specifiers, and X-bar Theory." in M. Baltin and A. Kroch (eds.) *Alternative Conceptions of Phrase Structure*, 232–262. Chicago: University of Chicago Press.

Strawson, P. (1952). *Introduction to Logical Theory*. London: Methuen.

Stump, G. T. (1985). *The Semantic Variability of Absolute Constructions.* Dordrecht: Reidel.

Swart, H. de (1991). "Adverbs of Quantification: A Generalized Quantifier Approach." Ph.D. dissertation, Rijksuniversiteit Groningen.

Szabolcsi, A. (1986). "From the Definiteness Effect to Lexical Integrity." In W. Abraham and S. de Mey (eds.) *Topic, Focus, and Configurationality*, 321–348. Amsterdam: John Benjamins.

Tappe, H.-T. (1989). "A Note on Split Topicalization in German." In C. Bhatt, E. Löbel, and C. Schmidt (eds.) *Syntactic Phrase Structure Phenomena in Noun Phrases and Sentences*, 157–179. Amsterdam: John Benjamins.

Tateishi, K. (1989). "Subjects, SPEC, and DP in Japanese." In *Proceedings of NELS 19*, 405–418. GLSA, University of Massachusetts, Amherst.

Tateishi, K. (1991). "The S-Structure Syntax of the Subject and 'S-Adjunctions'." Ph.D. dissertation, University of Massachusetts, Amherst.

Thiersch, C. (1978). "Topics in German Syntax." Ph.D. dissertation, MIT.

Vainikka, A. (1988). "Reply to Belletti." Ms., University of Massachusetts, Amherst.

Vainikka, A. (1989). "Deriving Syntactic Representations in Finnish." Ph.D. dissertation, University of Massachusetts, Amherst.

Vendler, Z. (1967). *Linguistics in Philosophy.* Ithaca, N.Y.: Cornell University Press.

Verhagen, A. (1986). *Linguistic Theory and the Function of Word Order in Dutch.* Dordrecht: Foris.

Wasow, T. (1979). *Anaphora in Generative Grammar.* Ghent: E. Story-Scientia.

Webelhuth, G. (1985). "German Is Configurational." *The Linguistic Review* 4, 203–246.

Webelhuth, G. (1989). "Syntactic Saturation Phenomena and the Modern Germanic Languages." Ph.D. dissertation, University of Massachusetts, Amherst.

Wexler, K., and P. W. Culicover (1980). *Formal Principles of Language Acquisition.* Cambridge, Mass.: MIT Press.

Wilkinson, K. (1986). "Generic Indefinite NPs." Ms., University of Massachusetts, Amherst.

Williams, E. (1977). "Discourse and Logical Form." *Linguistic Inquiry* 8, 101–139.

Williams, E. (1981). "Argument Structure and Morphology." *The Linguistic Review* 1, 81–114.

Williams, E. (1983). "Against Small Clauses." *Linguistic Inquiry* 14, 287–308.

Williams, E. (1986). "A Reassignment of the Functions of LF." *Linguistic Inquiry* 17, 265–299.

Williams, E. (1988). "Is LF Distinct from S-Structure? A Reply to May." *Linguistic Inquiry* 19, 135–146.

Wyngaerd, G. van den (1989). "Object Shift as an A-Movement Rule." In P. Branigan, J. Gaulding, M. Kubo, and K. Murasugi (eds.) *MIT Working Papers in Linguistics Volume 11: Student Conference in Linguistics 1989*, 256–271. Department of Linguistics and Philosophy, MIT.

Zubizarreta, M. L. (1982). "On the Relationship of the Lexicon to the Syntax." Ph.D. dissertation, MIT.

Zwarts, J. (1990). "Weak and Strong Noun Phrases and the DP-Hypothesis." To appear in *First LCJL Proceedings*. Rijksuniversiteit Groningen.

Index